ISS

L

D1461744

ISSUES
OF
LAW

CHARLES G. BLAKE

BBC PUBLICATIONS

This book accompanies the BBC
Television series *Issues of Law*
first broadcast on BBC 2 from
23 September 1986. The series
was produced by Tony Roberts.

Published to accompany a series of
programmes prepared in consultation
with the BBC Continuing Education
Advisory Council.

Published by BBC Publications,
a division of BBC Enterprises Ltd,
35 Marylebone High Street,
London WIM 4AA

ISBN: 0 563 21202 0

Typeset in 10/11 Bembo Linotron 202
by Rowland Phototypesetting Ltd,
Bury St Edmunds, Suffolk.
Printed and bound in England by
Mackays, Chatham, Kent.

Cover printed by Fletcher and Son,
Norwich.

CONTENTS

PREFACE

This book grew out of my involvement as a consultant to a BBC Television series on the legal system, also called *Issues of Law*. There is no shortage of books on the substantive rules of law and some of these are written for a general audience. But there are few works in print which take a broader view of the legal system, and the current turmoil affecting the legal profession makes the need for such a book all the greater. The aim of my book is to draw attention to the main features of the legal process and the range of legal services offered to the public. It raises more questions than it answers. Where necessary, it does not shrink from controversy.

After many years of static existence the legal profession is in the middle of a period of rapid change and some of what I have to say may be overtaken by events. I have tried to use materials available up to Easter 1986, and have mainly written about the legal system in England and Wales, which I know best; there are significant differences in Scotland and Northern Ireland.

I would like to thank my colleague Michael Molyneux (who was actively concerned in the production of the TV series) for his help and advice while writing this book. Tony Roberts, the producer of the series, also gave me much of his time and energies. Jennie Allen at BBC Publications was an excellent editor. Anne Frankel patiently turned my manuscript into perfect copy and Alison Baker put up with a lot of inconvenience while I was writing. Countless others – my former teachers (especially the late and greatly missed Professor Harry Street), my students and clients – have helped to shape my thoughts over many years.

Charles Blake
All Fool's Day, 1986

CHAPTER
1

INTRODUCTION

This book is about the law. Not so much about the rules or content of the law but rather the uses and expectations people have of the law in the United Kingdom today. I will be concerned not only with individuals, companies and public bodies that use the law every day but also with those to whom the law (and lawyers) are remote, of little apparent use and of even less interest. Generally I will be looking at civil and not at criminal law.

First I will examine the legal system as it exists today. This will not just be a guided tour of the courts. It will cover all our legal institutions and the personnel who operate within them. It will show how the system works, who uses it and how it might be better used to meet the needs of a society beset with economic and social problems. As with all social institutions that have a long history, development has been slow and there is a constant tension between the origins of a particular part of the system and its operation in a modern context.

The Legal System

The first problem to be faced is one of definition. What do we mean by 'the legal system'? Obviously it includes the courts, the lawyers who work within them (judges, barristers and solicitors) and the personnel employed within the courts to arrange the hearing of cases and to process the millions of pieces of paper generated by and within litigious procedures. But why stop there? Much modern law comes from the legislative activities of governments. Some of this law takes the form not only of Acts of Parliament but also of delegated legislation. This is detailed rule-making left to government departments because Parliament does not have the time to deal with the complexities of modern regulatory laws. For example, the details of supplementary benefit law are contained in about two hundred pages of complex and often impenetrable regulations. At the end of 1985 about seven million people (claimants and their dependants) were dependent in whole or in part on this means of financial support. About 70,000 staff work in social security offices all over the country and are responsible for handling claims. Here is an example of the present state of the regulations:

► *Determination of amount of water charges*

5B.—(1) Where a housing requirement in respect of water charges is applicable to the claimant, and—

(*a*) the amount of his other requirements, as determined under the Requirements Regulations, exceeds the amount of his resources, as calculated in accordance with the Resources Regulations, by not less than the minimum amount of supplementary benefit payable in accordance with regulation 10(1) or, as the case may be, (2) of the Supplementary Benefit (Claims and Payments) Regulations 1981(**a**);

(*b*) he is, apart from this regulation, entitled to supplementary benefit, and regulation 9 of the Housing Benefits Regulations 1982 (certificated cases) will apply to him;

► (*c*) the water charges—

(i) are collected direct from the claimant or his partner by an authority (being, in relation to England and Wales, a housing authority within the meaning of section 35(1) of the Social Security and Housing Benefits Act 1982(**b**) and, in relation to Scotland, a housing or rating authority within the meaning of that section 35(1)) on behalf of the water authority or water company or, in Scotland, on behalf of a regional or islands council which is a water authority, or

(ii) are included in rent part of which is eligible for a rent allowance from a local authority under the Housing Benefits Regulations 1982, ► and are collected direct from the claimant or his partner by the landlord, ◄ ◄

the benefit officer shall determine that the amount of pension or allowance payable shall be the amount of the excess plus the amount which the Secretary of State shall determine to be applicable in respect of water charges.

(2) Written notice of a determination made by the Secretary of State under paragraph (1) shall not be required except at the request of the claimant.

(3) In this regulation "water charges" means any charge or rate mentioned in regulation 19(1)(*a*) of the Requirements Regulations (water and, except in Scotland, sewerage and allied environmental services). ◄

At first sight this regulation is almost incomprehensible. It seems to deal with payments for 'water charges' but requires reference to be made to numerous other sets of regulations to be interpreted properly. The key words are in fact 'the amount of the excess' because it is this sum that is paid to the claimant and is all the claimant cares about. 'Excess' over what? To discover that it is necessary to look at another regulation which, in turn, involves taking account of concepts derived from yet other regulations. Here we have problems of language, interpretation and application of words to individual cases as complex as any other problem likely to be faced by the courts. But the point is that disputes about the application of such regulations do not (initially at any rate) go before the courts. They are first decided by Adjudication Officers in local social security offices. They are conscientious civil servants often working with an impossible case load. But they have no legal training and have to interpret the words which were drafted (probably at great speed) by a lawyer employed by the Department of Health and Social Security.

There is a mechanism for resolving disputes about the meaning of the regulations which involves a hearing before a tribunal. The chairman will almost invariably be a lawyer. (Tribunals will be dealt with in more detail in Chapter Two.) The point of this complicated tale is to show that those who use the law are not restricted to the personnel of the court system. Probably the Adjudication Officer will not refer to the wording of the regulation. Recent research by the Chief Adjudication Officer shows that many local offices do not have access to an up-to-date set of the regulations. Instead they will rely on internal DHSS manuals (which may also not be up to date) which summarise and re-state the law in more ordinary English. As for the claimant, he or she will almost certainly not have access to either the original regulations or to the DHSS manual although both are on sale – at great cost. Possibly a local Citizens' Advice Bureau or law centre will have access to both the regulations and the manual and, in addition, could provide expert advice. A local firm of solicitors would be most unlikely to have any knowledge of the relevant law.

Using the Law

Take another example. Most hazardous enterprises are subject to a form of regulation which may involve supervision of activities by either a local or a central form of inspectorate. At the basis of the inspector's activities will lie a complex body of regulations sometimes specifying in great detail what is or is not permissible and sometimes leaving a great deal of discretion to the inspector. In either case the enterprise subject to regulation will have to acquire, through its employees, a working knowledge of the relevant law. Few such employees will have a legal training. Nor will the inspectors be lawyers although they will be very conversant with the regulations. Lying behind the daily contact between inspector and inspected is not only the law itself but also the possibility of legal action to enforce the regulations. In practice the formal mechanism of the law is rarely invoked and reliance is placed on negotiations between both parties to produce an operational level of compliance with the law that is satisfactory. What this commonplace experience shows is that the law may be used, bargained about and, on occasions, ignored in favour of some lesser or more practicable standard. Each of those who participate in the process of bargaining will have his or her own perception of the law and of its importance. And any study of the legal system which concentrates solely on formal institutions and the work of lawyers will miss much of what is valuable and interesting about the way the law is used.

Some broader examples may reinforce this point. If we look at a daily newspaper (at least, at one usually referred to as part of the 'quality press') we can see how pervasive the law has become in our society. There will be leading stories that involve, at the simplest level, reports or summaries of what has happened in some current court case. Usually it will be a criminal case involving either large scale fraud or a particularly brutal crime of violence. (Local newspapers often seem to be composed of a tedious list of almost every criminal case heard in the local Magistrates' Court but our concern is much wider.) Then there will be political stories often involving a proposal for new legislation on a particular topic. Whether the law can solve every social or political problem is a question we can postpone for the moment but it is perceived by both politicians and many of the public as having that function.

The foreign news pages often carry stories about negotiations between states which may result in formal treaties. These form part of a complex body of rules known as international law although few lawyers have any detailed knowledge of, or need to have an interest in, its operation and working. Beyond this it may seem to the reader that little of what remains involves the law.

But this is not so. Take the following head-lines to items which appeared in *The Times* for one day towards the end of 1985.

'Norwich Board Quit'
(The board of directors of Norwich City football club – run as a limited company – resigned after an argument about the relationship of one director to the firm which was awarded the contract to rebuild the main stand. This raises questions of company law, the law of contract and, as a board of trustees was appointed to run the club temporarily, the law of trusts.)

'Brassey Inquiry Date Set'
(The Jockey Club planned to start disciplinary proceedings against a trainer who withdrew a horse at a late stage from a race. This meant that the weights carried by other horses – designed to give outside runners a slightly better chance of getting into the leading runners – could not be adjusted in time. This raises questions about the interpretation of the Jockey Club's rules, their legal status and the procedures followed by the Club in disciplinary hearings.)

'Bid Fever Adds £952m to Shares Value'
(Take-over bids have great consequences for employees, shareholders and the market in which the companies in question operate. They are regulated by a mixture of complex company law, contract law and internal rules of the Stock Exchange.)

This is enough to show that we live, not so much in a legalistic or litigious society, but in a society of a complex nature with much law affecting, perhaps indirectly, our lives and those of our employers, friends, family and the public and private bodies with which we deal from day to day. We do not need to know very much about the law in order to live our lives. Nobody knows all of the law. But we do need to be aware of how and why the law impinges on our lives.

The Courts

Having seen that the legal system is an intangible, general and wide-reaching form of control, regulation or effect on ourselves we can return to an examination of its more tangible features. First we can consider the courts and their general function. At this stage we need not draw clear distinctions between civil and criminal law and civil and criminal courts. There is a great deal of overlap between their respective functions. In general terms the purpose of the law is to protect major interests which are respected in our society. First amongst these is the protection of property rights. These take an enormous variety of forms. Some are obvious such as the ownership of a home, a television set or a work of art. Others are less visible such as copyright in a plan, diagram or drawing. Some writers argue that social security benefits are a form of property right. Much of what is usually called 'private law' concerns the regulation, transfer and protection of property interests. The number of cases that actually reach a hearing on such matters today are few but the influence of the law is very great. Its rules are generally well known by lawyers who can safely advise their clients and process business arrangements. Beyond this property rights include the right to enforce payments for goods or services sold on credit. The phenomenal growth of credit in the last twenty years has both economic and legal implications. Coupled with a growth in unemployment many problems of inability to pay are produced. Much of the work of the civil courts is taken up with claims by creditors against individuals or small businesses who have not paid what they owe.

The criminal courts are also concerned with the protection of property interests. Theft, burglary, criminal damage are all crimes against property and take up a large amount of the time of the Magistrates' Court and Crown Court. In addition the courts are concerned with crimes of violence (sometimes linked with crimes against property) and a host of regulatory offences notably in relation to motoring.

A more useful distinction than between civil and criminal courts is one between the various users of the judicial machinery provided by the state. We can distinguish between individuals, companies, public bodies and the government itself.

Individuals are most commonly defendants in claims for money due brought by companies. As most such claims are for less than £5,000 they are usually brought in the County Court. These are local courts situated in medium and large sized towns with a number of courts in central and suburban London. Not only is their jurisdiction limited in financial terms but they also can only hear cases where the claim arises because the person who is sued lives within the district of the court. Alternatively the events leading to the case will have happened within the district of the court. This avoids that person incurring travel costs in attending a hearing in a remote court. Where individuals bring actions themselves they usually do so because they want to claim compensation for personal injuries suffered at work, or more often, in a road traffic accident. Sometimes they wish to make claims against sellers of faulty or shoddy goods or suppliers (often builders) of poor quality services. With increasing frequency they bring proceedings to terminate marriages and to sort out the financial consequences of divorces and who should have custody of any children.

It is not common to find individuals litigating in the higher courts except for large claims for compensation for personal injury. And when they do bring claims they are usually based on disputes as to fact rather than as to the law. For example, a claim for compensation based on injuries received in a road traffic accident will rarely raise any issue of law. The law of negligence on which such a claim would be based is very clear. It requires the person injured to prove that the other driver was at fault. The claim will be defended by the driver's insurance company and the chief problem the injured person will have will be the proof of fault. For example, the defence may suggest that the accident occurred because a tyre was defectively manufactured and exploded causing the driver to lose control of the car. This may raise very difficult questions of fact, evidence and proof. (Whether our lawyers are always adept at obtaining such proof will be considered in Chapter Two.) No great legal knowledge is required to bring or defend such a case although, as we shall see, the skills in which lawyers are trained are not always directed towards the needs of such clients.

Using the Courts

Business interests appear much more frequently in the higher courts. They claim money due above £5,000 which often results from (or in) a dispute about goods delivered or services supplied. In addition companies are often nominal parties to actions brought by or against insurance companies. In one case a security guard had, for a reason which was never discovered, lit a fire at one of the factories in his charge. It burnt down causing loss of business as well as physical destruction. Which insurer had to bear the ultimate loss – the company that had insured the building or the company that had insured the legal liability of the firm providing the security guard? In the end the courts decided that an exclusion clause in the security contract was effective and the loss had to be met by the property insurers. Similar cases arise where goods prove to be faulty and cause loss of profit. Another example would be where damage is caused by flooding and, the property insurers having met the claim, there is litigation between them and, say, the neighbouring landowners who caused the flooding.

A common source of commercial litigation is a dispute about land. This might take the form of an argument about the terms of a contract to buy or sell land. More commonly the power of the courts may be invoked to interpret the meaning and application of the words of a lease of land. (A lease is simply a grant of possession of land by one person to another in return for the payment of rent.) Leases are getting longer and longer and there is ample scope for dispute as to what the words might mean. There is a lot of evidence that where businesses are in frequent contact with each other and have a long-term interest in not terminating their continuing relationship, then resorting to court proceedings may not be very likely. This does not seem to apply with so much force where the dispute is about rent or some other financial aspect of a dealing in land.

Naturally businesses do bring legal proceedings where relationships have broken down entirely or where there is a large amount of money at stake. Such cases vary from disputes about the meaning of commercial contracts to complex legal questions that concern insurance law, banking practices or the legal consequences of careless advice or badly prepared accounts. Also businesses may find that an arbitration procedure may lead to court action. Arbitration is a favoured way of resolving commercial disputes. It avoids the publicity and delay often associated with court procedures. The decision can be made speedily by an expert in the particular field. The danger is that the expert (usually not a lawyer) may make a mistake of law and the case may then be referred to the High Court. Since the Arbitration Act of 1979 the circumstances in which the courts may intervene have been severely restricted. London has always been an important centre for both domestic and international arbitrations and the ease with which the courts could be brought into arbitrations was causing disquiet among business interests. The speed and efficiency of the arbitration process were threatened by applications made to the courts for points of law to be decided. The broader question is how far informal and self-regulating processes of justice should be encouraged or restricted. I will return to this in Chapter Two.

The Courts at Work

At this stage it may be helpful to have a more complete picture
of the court system at work. The diagram on page 18 shows the
system of civil courts. It will be seen that the main disposal of
cases takes place in the County Court where most defendants do
not defend the proceedings, and judgment is obtained in default of
such participation. There is cause for concern in many such cases
because defences of one sort or another can often be found. For
example, the provision of consumer credit is subject to detailed
regulation and failure to comply with formalities may lead to
an agreement being unenforceable. In the County Court there
is neither time nor the facility to investigate every claim to see
whether it is or is not well founded. Our system of litigation is
adversarial. That is, it requires each party to make out its case and
to establish the basis for a claim (or a defence) both in fact and in
law. This usually requires legal representation or, at least, access
to some kind of legal advice. We will see later why relatively few
defendants do seek legal advice. The attitude of County Court
judges and registrars (broadly these are lesser judges) towards
unrepresented or absent claimants varies enormously. Some will
take great pains to see whether a claim is justified. Other will take
the defendant's absence to indicate an admission of liability. In
most cases of simple debt a failure to respond to the proceedings
(usually served by post) will lead to a judgment being obtained
automatically. The court does not investigate in any way the
validity of a claim when it is presented. The point to notice is
that the legal system would barely operate at its present cost
and level of efficiency if every defendant were represented or if
every defendant appeared at court hearings and required strict
proof of a claim.

Whether a case is heard in the County Court or in the High
Court the simple fact is that of the millions of cases begun each
year only a tiny number are heard formally by a judge. Even if the
defendant indicates in response to the formal proceedings that he
or she wishes to defend, there exist mechanisms for bringing cases
to a speedy conclusion if no real defence exists. These are most
commonly used in the High Court although a similar procedure
exists in the County Court. This is a very necessary process but,
as it can happen very quickly, it again points to the need for
adequate legal advice to be readily available.

The higher courts hear relatively few cases. The Court of
Appeal hears appeals (almost entirely limited to points of law)

CIVIL COURTS

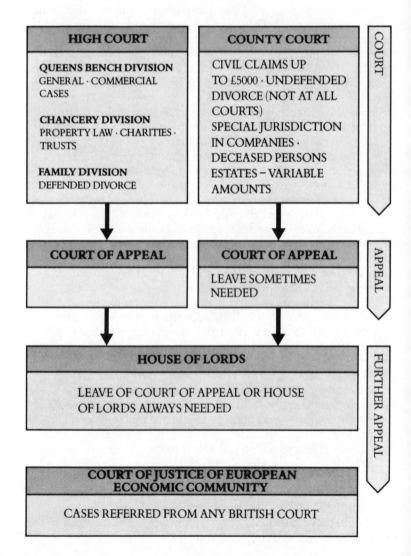

HIGH COURT	COUNTY COURT	COURT
QUEENS BENCH DIVISION GENERAL · COMMERCIAL CASES **CHANCERY DIVISION** PROPERTY LAW · CHARITIES · TRUSTS **FAMILY DIVISION** DEFENDED DIVORCE	CIVIL CLAIMS UP TO £5000 · UNDEFENDED DIVORCE (NOT AT ALL COURTS) SPECIAL JURISDICTION IN COMPANIES · DECEASED PERSONS ESTATES – VARIABLE AMOUNTS	

COURT OF APPEAL	COURT OF APPEAL	APPEAL
	LEAVE SOMETIMES NEEDED	

HOUSE OF LORDS	FURTHER APPEAL
LEAVE OF COURT OF APPEAL OR HOUSE OF LORDS ALWAYS NEEDED	

COURT OF JUSTICE OF EUROPEAN ECONOMIC COMMUNITY
CASES REFERRED FROM ANY BRITISH COURT

from both the High Court and the County Court. In recent years the court has been concerned to speed up the hearing of appeals and, as a means of doing so, to limit the circumstances in which it will overturn the judgment of a lower court. It does this by holding that it will very rarely interfere with what it terms the use of discretion by the lower court. For example, suppose that a person is awarded damages for personal injuries by a court which heard the evidence and reached a reasoned conclusion. Unless that person can show that the award is far too low the Court of Appeal will say that the lower judge had a discretion, proceeded to exercise it and that must be an end of the matter. Of course this can work both ways. It may operate to the advantage of a claimant where the award is higher than usual but not so high as to be excessive. What then is the function of the Court of Appeal if it can often be said that a lower decision involved a discretion and was not wholly wrong? It does have a role in dealing with difficult points of law. Increasingly these are points of interpretation of statute law. Some such points will affect large numbers of people. For example the term 'income' in tax legislation has never been fully or conclusively defined by that legislation. This may seem strange given that all those in employment are likely to have to pay income tax. Against this there may be good reasons for not adopting a close definition of what is intended to be a broad concept and contrasted with 'capital' which is itself not fully defined. To take another example from the criminal law, to be guilty of theft it is essential that the taking of the item is accompanied by a dishonest state of mind. 'Dishonesty' is not fully defined by the Theft Act, 1968 which was designed to modernise the law and the courts have not supplied a definition of their own preferring to leave the question to be decided in each case by magistrates or by a jury applying commonly accepted standards.

The Court of Appeal does have the task of examining the legal content of decisions of the lower courts as opposed to exercises of discretion although the process is fluid and is itself an expression of the discretion of the Court of Appeal. In cases that do not involve statutory interpretation it must look at the decision in question and decide whether the lower court was right or wrong in law. This is not an easy task. It involves an examination of all relevant earlier cases, deciding what principle they establish and how, if at all, that principle should be applied to the facts of the present case. It cannot generally reopen the lower decision on the facts. It will be rare for the law to be so clear as to admit of no doubt or difficulty and, very often, it is in a state to allow the Court of Appeal to take either view urged on it by the parties to the case and to be able to justify it in terms of legal doctrine. The court is only bound to follow its own previous decisions and those of the House of Lords but differences between past and present cases can usually be found to justify not slavishly adhering to the past. This is not to say that the law is arbitrary or so broad as to be unknown. It is merely to point out that the law is difficult to state with precision and it is up to the parties to litigation either to reach an agreement between themselves or to litigate and possibly to contribute to the future development of the law in that area.

For an example of a decision of the Court of Appeal on a commonplace event see the judgments in *Ward* v. *Tesco Stores Ltd* in the appendix to this book. Notice that the case has a 'headnote' summarising the facts and the decision, that it says who gave the judgments and who were the barristers and solicitors. It also says which previous cases were referred to. One judge dissented so the decision was given by a majority of two to one. The decision is not only important for supermarkets. It would (and still does) cover any occupier of a building or land – such as a garage forecourt – where a danger occurs that is not dealt with promptly.

The House of Lords is the highest court and in civil matters only hears about thirty cases each year. These tend to fall into three main groups. First, there are cases on tax where complex points of statutory interpretation may arise. In these instances costs are usually no object compared with the amount at stake and the case is lavishly argued with great reference to previous cases. Second, there is a series of cases on difficult points of judge-made law such as the law of negligence. This is an example of an area of legal development where the principles are easy enough to state but hard to apply in practice. 'Negligence' simply means not taking proper care in day-to-day activities to look after the interests of others who are affected by what we do or fail to do. This gives rise to very difficult problems. Does liability extend to all losses that occur or is there some limit? How is lack of care to be measured? If the harm which occurs does not cause personal injury but only economic loss must that be paid for by the person not taking care (or the insurers) or is it better to leave the injured party to take out insurance? These questions may not be very important for most individuals. Their prime impact is on insurance companies trying to estimate their future liabilities.

In such cases the decisions of the House of Lords are not easy to follow. The judgments (technically called 'speeches') are discursive, lengthy and often puzzling to lawyers. It is rare to find every point that arose in the case being answered. Many matters are left over for future decision. This is probably the best that can be achieved because there is little political interest in such areas of law and no government will take time to legislate on questions where no more can be done than to lay down broad principles for application in future cases.

The third category of case is that of attempts made to challenge the legality of central or local governmental action. This is called 'judicial review'. It is one of the more controversial areas of law and has developed rapidly in recent years. It is, in essence, a simple notion. The theory is that government can only act in accordance with the law. This means that a Minister or local authority can only act within the powers conferred upon that office or function either by Act of Parliament or in accordance with what remains of implied powers that the central state has deriving from the ancient royal prerogative.

Judicial Review of Governmental Action

Any exercise of power by central or local government must not only conform to the powers of the individual or body concerned but must also be exercised in a lawful way. Over the last thirty years the courts have developed a number of general principles by which the use of powers has to be measured. Even if the powers are discretionary in nature (that is, the government 'may' do something if it wishes but it is not bound to do so) some judicial control can be exerted. The principles may be summed up in this way. When exercising a power a public body must:

a direct itself correctly on the law;
b take account of relevant factors when making a decision;
c not take account of irrelevant factors;
d not act so unreasonably that no reasonable public body could possibly have come to such a conclusion.

These are very general notions and it is not always easy to apply them to individual cases. Moreover it is a very controversial jurisdiction because it brings the courts into the political arena and may lead to accusations of partiality as between political choices which might be best left to elected bodies. In other words what are issues of politics and economics cannot and should not be presented as issues of law. Politicians may get the answers wrong but are responsible to the electorate unlike the judges who are appointed.

Professor John Griffith argues strongly that the growth of judicial review over discretionary powers leaves too much power to the judges. In his brilliant polemical work *The Politics of the Judiciary* (Fontana, 1985) he contends that the very general nature of the principles of judicial review allows judges to make policy decisions which he considers strongly conservative in nature and opposed to modern welfare legislation. This debate continues and it is interesting to note that since the present government's election in 1979 it has fallen foul of the courts on numerous occasions and ministers have found that they did not have the powers they thought they had.

Some Examples of Judicial Review

Two examples of the use of the law to challenge the acts of public bodies will help to explain the controversy highlighted by Griffith. In 1976 the then Labour government wanted to persuade or, if that failed, to compel those education authorities that had not introduced comprehensive schools to do so without delay. In May of that year Tameside council (an area on the edge of Manchester) passed into Conservative control and decided to implement plans to maintain selective education. Curiously there was no Act of Parliament which said they had to introduce a comprehensive scheme. The Department of Education and Science had preferred to rely on persuasion and financial incentives to change.

In this one case, however, the Minister, Mr Mulley, decided that he would act under powers contained in the 1944 Education Act. Section 68 allowed him to give directions to a local authority if he was 'satisfied' that the authority intended to 'act unreasonably with respect to the exercise of any power'. The Minister decided that it was unreasonable for Tameside to continue selective education. He directed them to introduce a comprehensive scheme. When the council declined to comply the Minister took legal proceedings to compel them to do so on the basis that they were bound, in law, to follow his direction.

Tameside argued that the Minister had no power in law to issue his direction. The case went to the House of Lords. It decided that the Minister was wrong to issue a direction. This was not because the courts wished to become involved in a political dispute nor because they wished to substitute their view of what a good system of education would be for the Minister's opinion. What they did say was that the Minister had misdirected himself in law. On the facts of the political dispute the Minister was wrong to be 'satisfied' that the council was acting 'unreasonably' because he did not consider whether the selective education preferred by Tameside could be operated by the time the autumn term in 1976 began. The House of Lords maintained that it was not concerned with the merits of the issue but only with the legality of the Minister's actions. Put another way the Minister's discretion was not absolute. He could not be 'satisfied' about something in law unless the factual basis for his 'satisfaction' existed.

Some commentators claimed that whatever it said the House of Lords was interfering in a political dispute and that it had no right to do so. This argument was taken up with greater force in 1982. The Greater London Council (now abolished) implemented a promise in the election manifesto of the Labour group in 1981 that it would reduce bus and underground fares by one quarter. It wanted to achieve this by increasing the grant to the London Transport Executive. This grant was financed by a levy on all London boroughs. However it would cause the rate level to rise above a government set threshold in a 1980 Act of Parliament. This meant that central government grants would be lost. Bromley Council, a Conservative controlled outer London borough, challenged the GLC's action. It claimed that the GLC had no power to levy such a rate.

The main argument for Bromley was that the power of the GLC to reduce fares was beyond the law. An Act passed in 1969 gave the GLC power to develop 'integrated' and 'economic transport facilities in London'. Examining the Act as a whole the GLC took account of what it thought was its general duty to act responsibly towards ratepayers. These existed independently of the specific legislation relating to London Transport and the creation of an integrated system of transport in Greater London. Ultimately the House of Lords decided that the GLC had no power to act as it had because it had not given sufficient weight to the need to avoid losing central government grants nor had it evaluated properly the respective interests of the ratepayers and passengers – not all passengers were ratepayers nor were all ratepayers passengers.

At one level it is easy enough to say that this was a policy or even a political decision disguised as a piece of complex legal reasoning. It can also be argued that local government can only act in accordance with its powers and that if an Act of Parliament does not clearly indicate what powers exist then the courts have to interpret the Act as best they can. Naturally views on the meaning of ambiguous words may differ. This may result in a situation where the power of the courts to review discretionary decisions of the executive is itself discretionary and is not based on any clear or precise rules. But governments are (or should be) well aware of the body of law which was built up in this area (usually called 'public' or 'administrative' law) and can, if they wish, make clearer provision in Acts of Parliament as to what are the legal implications of policy decisions made by themselves and local government.

In any case there is much about judicial review that is not controversial. The courts have, by using the broad concept of 'natural justice', imposed duties of fair decision-making on bodies which have the power to grant or take away licences or control someone's career. In 1963 the House of Lords held that a local police committee could not dismiss a Chief Constable without giving him a chance to state his case. It could not just rely on adverse comments made about him at a criminal trial. This opened the way for many decisions which have required public bodies to introduce proper procedures for appointing and dismissing employees and for taking decisions generally in pursuit of their statutory powers.

The most recent example of an interesting use of judicial review was an application by the Chairman of the Bar Council against the Lord Chancellor. The Bar, in an unprecedented move, claimed that the five per cent increase on criminal aid fees which had been offered to criminal practitioners was unlawful. It based its case on the 'legitimate expectation' which had been created by an assurance that negotiations would proceed. The Lord Chancellor was compelled to ask for the case to be adjourned for several months to negotiate further with the Bar as the court strongly hinted that it would find against him. The evidence showed that the Bar's expectation of negotiations was reasonably based on correspondence it had received, although the Lord Chancellor had to admit that he intended to offer five per cent only at a time when the Bar believed there would be further discussions. Of course the High Court cannot decide how much barristers should be paid. But it was able to suggest inadequacies within the Lord Chancellor's negotiating procedures. The other significant feature of the case is the very fact that it was brought. A few years ago it would have been unthinkable for the Bar to challenge a decision by the Lord Chancellor. Such are the pressures upon some barristers that the unthinkable has become quite acceptable. Incidentally the Law Society also obtained a promise of further negotiations on legal aid remuneration having brought its own case for judicial review, which was promptly adjourned once the Bar had achieved some degree of success.

Judicial review is a growing area of decision-making by judges. It is surrounded by a number of safeguards for statutory bodies. An action must normally be brought within three months of the decision complained about. Before proceedings can commence the leave of the court must be obtained. This is done by preparing a statement of the facts sworn on oath (called an affidavit) which indicates what act of illegality is complained of. There are restrictions on those who can complain to the courts in that some individual interest in the allegedly illegal act has to be demonstrated before the court will hear the case. These are called the laws of 'standing'. Moreover judicial review is not like an appeal. It is only concerned with the legality of executive action and not with its merits. For example, someone may complain that a local authority should have classified him as a homeless person and therefore he should have been rehoused under an Act of Parliament requiring authorities to rehouse at least some homeless people. If the court agrees and decides, say, that the local authority misdirected itself in law as to what 'homeless' means or failed to make proper inquiries into a person's status as homeless it can only overturn the adverse decision. It cannot give the complainant a home – only the local authority can do that. What it can do is to say where and why the authority went wrong and leave it to make a fresh decision.

Controversy will continue to rage about the proper extent of judicial review and the proper role of the courts. The present state of the law gives great scope to the judges to intervene in executive decisions and the balance between the merits and legality of a decision is never easy to state. We shall return to this topic in the final chapter looking at arguments for and against the introduction of a Bill of Rights.

Other Courts

There are some other developments in the judicial system which

are less well known. First, there is the growing importance of the
law of the European Economic Communities. Since 1973 when
Britain joined the EEC it has usually been thought that EEC law
is only of concern to big business and farmers. More recently
lawyers have come to see that it may affect day-to-day aspects of
commercial life. EEC law is primarily concerned to establish the
framework for a free market in goods, services, labour and capital. It strikes at all sorts of restrictive practices and restrictions on
employment of EEC nationals. It is possible for an English court
to refer to the EEC court in Luxembourg questions of interpretation of EEC law. In some cases a reference must be made –
notably when the House of Lords is deciding a case on a difficult
point of EEC law. The Luxembourg court (which is composed of
one judge from each member state) has to decide what the
relevant piece of EEC law means. It is then for the English courts
to apply this ruling to the facts of the case. As the interest and
concerns of the EEC extend into more and more areas of life we
may see greater use made of the ability to refer cases to the
Luxembourg court. Increasingly UK lawyers are finding that
they may fail in their duty to their clients unless they take account
of EEC law. Some recent cases in negligence have been brought
against lawyers who did not know of relevant EEC law when
advising on value-added tax.

Finally, we have the system of protecting human rights in
Europe. This is a complex and rather slow process. Britain is a
signatory to the European Convention on Human Rights and it
also recognises the right of individuals to bring claims against it
before the Commission of Human Rights in Strasbourg. The
Convention is written in very general terms, unlike English law
which usually specifies rights in precise language. For example,
one provision reads: 'Everyone has the right to respect for his
private and family life, his home and correspondence'. Then
there is a proviso which allows interference with such rights
where (amongst other possibilities) 'it is necessary in a democratic
society for . . . the protection of health or morals or for the
protection of the rights and freedoms of others'.

Clearly such general concepts can command broad agreement
by European states leaving their precise meaning and application
to be worked out later. Because the Convention is not part of
English law anyone in this country who wishes to challenge an
existing law or administrative practice must do so first by ex-
hausting all rights before English courts or tribunals and then by

bringing a complaint before the Commission. This is a very slow process as the Commission is composed of part-time members and receives many complaints. It first decides whether any basis for a breach of the Convention exists. If it decides that there is no such basis it declares the complaint 'inadmissible' and that is the end of the matter. If it decides that a complaint has some basis it declares it 'admissible' and then tries to bring about a friendly settlement between the individual and the state concerned. If this is not successful the case will usually be referred to the Court of Human Rights (which is made up of judges from almost every West European state). It has to decide what the Convention means (and it will look at its own previous decisions in order to do so) and whether there has been a breach in the present case. If there has then English law is not automatically changed but the government has an obligation to change the law to bring it into line with the Convention. Recent examples are challenges to the Home Secretary's powers to order telephones to be tapped, procedures for regulating prisons and measures of immigration control. In each case the United Kingdom's laws and practices have been found wanting and have been changed in accordance with the decision of the Court. Awareness of the Court's real powers has been an important feature of the development of legal rights in this country in recent years.

CHAPTER
2

THE LITIGATION PROCESS AND
ITS EFFECTS

The point has already been made that to focus solely on formal court procedures is to misunderstand and misstate the nature of the legal system. Because much of a lawyer's work is not concerned with litigation (or any type of dispute) it is important to know not only how the formal system works and how its human agents operate it but also what shadow it casts over the remaining legal mechanism. This chapter will look firstly at how formal dispute resolution works and, secondly, will assess what impact this has on the general provision of legal services.

Anyone with a dispute that is capable of resolution before the ordinary courts will inevitably require legal advice and assistance. So will many without a dispute but in need of legal services, for example, in relation to a commercial contract. For the moment we can assume that there is no problem about the cost of such services – this is so important that it is dealt with in Chapter Four. What we have to consider is who are the givers of advice, how do they organise and perceive their task and how likely is it that the advice given or service provided will be able to deal with the issues raised speedily and effectively? And how is it that our present legal structures came to be as they are?

The most obvious feature of the provision of legal services is that they are dominated by the private legal profession even though many of the services provided are paid for, wholly or in part, by the state under the legal aid and advice schemes. There are in practice about 46,000 solicitors and 5,300 barristers. The reasons for having a divided legal profession are now long lost in history. Arguments for fusion of the two are often raised but are not currently on any political agenda. Rather than rehearse them at length it may be more helpful to see exactly how solicitors and barristers are organised and what they actually do.

Solicitors at Work

Take solicitors first. They are the first line of communication between the public and the law – at any rate the non-criminal law. Their number has almost doubled in the last twenty years partly because of increased provision for the education of lawyers and partly because the inexorable encouragement of owner occupation has led to a greatly increased demand for their services in buying and selling property. Solicitors must practise within constraints laid down by their governing body, the Law Society. They must keep accurate and up-to-date accounts. They must keep their own money separate from that belonging to (or held by them for) their clients. They may now advertise their services but only in accordance with guidelines laid down by the Law Society. They may not practise in the form of a limited liability company as they must always be personally liable to their clients for money held for them. These rules are straightforward enough and are designed to protect the interests of clients against dishonest or wholly incompetent practitioners. We will not dwell here on the training and education of lawyers but rather on their practices.

Traditionally solicitors have served the interests of those wishing to buy or sell rights of property. The Royal Commission on Legal Services showed (in 1979) that about half of most solicitors' income came from conveyancing – that is from the legal work relating to the buying and selling of houses, flats and commercial properties. For many years solicitors have had an effective monopoly of such work (even though much of it was carried out by unqualified employees) and the Law Society frequently prosecuted those who broke the law. The argument in favour of the monopoly ranged from the disinterested ('it is necessary to restrict skilled and complex legal work to those able to carry it out effectively') to the somewhat crude ('without advertising we must be able to ensure a reasonable flow of profitable work in part to subsidise litigation which does not pay'). Change came rather rapidly. First, the requirement that all solicitors charge a prescribed fee for conveyancing (fixed by reference to the value of the property) was abandoned some fifteen years ago. This led to a certain degree of competition for conveyancing services. Second, the extension of the right to provide conveyancing services to a new type of practitioner is currently being implemented. A 'licensed conveyancer' will, after recognition by a new council set up for that purpose, be able to act in most transactions. This will undoubtedly lead to greater competition but as the educational requirements are likely to be quite oncrous it will be some years before licensed conveyancers have much impact on the cost of such services.

Apart from conveyancing services solicitors have historically derived another twenty per cent of their income from probate cases. That is, they have acted in the preparation of wills and later in the submission of the necessary papers to the courts to enable the executors (appointed under the will) to obtain a grant of probate and to have the right to act in dealing with the estate of the deceased person.

Solicitors and Litigation

This means that other services (advisory, litigious and negotiating with other parties) have traditionally not been a major source of a solicitor's income. Indeed they have often been subsidised by fees from property work. It should be noted that we are here concerned with medium or small sized firms of solicitors primarily dealing with private clients. There is also a small number of very large firms mainly congregated in the City of London or in other central London districts. Such firms may have over sixty partners with a total staff of over one thousand. Such firms will serve almost exclusively commercial and banking clients. They will provide an excellent service employing only the best educated lawyers and will make full use of modern technology – computers, word-processors, facsimile communication devices. They will only rarely act for individuals and they will charge fees in excess of £200 for each hour of work done. Much of their work will consist of dealing with other similar firms and negotiating contracts, terms for the takeover of companies, international financing agreements and other banking documents. They will also deal with substantial litigation of a commercial nature. Such firms are at the top of the profession in terms of competence, skill and the ability to serve their clients' interests in the most effective manner possible.

There is great demand among high quality law students for employment in such an environment. But it is hardly typical of much legal work undertaken in this country. Neither their methods nor their access to technical equipment nor their clientele represent anything but the most exceptional. Yet it should be the case that the quality of work undertaken by smaller firms is not significantly lower. Whether the education and training of lawyers is adequate for this task will be discussed separately. What we have to consider now is how the majority of small or medium sized firms carry out their work.

The first thing that the solicitor must do is to understand the client's problem and to see what steps can and should be taken immediately and in the longer term to protect the client's interest. This requires the display of a variety of skills – listening to the client, reading and understanding a set of documents, whether correspondence or contracts. It may require some instant action such as the obtaining of an injunction or filing papers with a court to prevent some adverse step being taken against the client. It is at this stage that the services of a barrister may be required. There are several reasons why such services may be needed, and many problems connected with them. In broad terms barristers have a monopoly of the rights of audience in the higher courts. But they are not merely specialist advocates (even if they were they have mostly received a poor training for this work as we will see). They are also supposed to have a more detailed and knowledge-able grasp of the relevant area of law. Some will be specialists in one or more fields of legal work. They will also have a thorough understanding of the rules of procedure which govern the conduct of litigation. Their main function will be to draft the formal documents required to state a case in the High or County Court. This is not just a single step. The papers will have to be returned to the barrister at frequent intervals throughout the case. This has been criticised as causing delay, needless additional expense and confusion for a client who sees one person but whose case is partly dealt with by another. There is a lot of force in these comments but, given that this is the system we have, it is more apposite to see whether in its actual operation the client suffers. Not always and not necessarily is the answer. A well prepared case will require constant contact between the barrister, the solicitor and the client. When this happens regularly and the case has been well prepared, then the system is at its most efficient because the specialisation that has been developed enables both the barrister and the solicitor to undertake their function efficiently. Thus the solicitor will primarily be responsible for obtaining and checking the facts. The barrister will primarily be responsible for knowing the relevant law and advising on the case as it develops. What causes needless difficulty is not so much the system itself but its poor operation. If, as often happens, preparation is left until too late, the facts are not checked at the beginning of the case or the barrister's advice is not followed, then the client has cause to be dissatisfied. It would be more convenient for the client to see one person (or at least one team of lawyers only), but the present system can be made to operate with a fair degree of efficiency accepting that work is to be divided up in this way.

The Lord Chancellor, Lord Hailsham, when asked about this point for the BBC Television series *Issues of Law* explained that:

> 'a solicitor . . . has an expensive office with rent and rates to pay, employing a large number of clerks, he has to pay his partners, he has to interview clients and his overheads are so high that he can't afford to wait about in court for his case to come on. A barrister on the other hand with his relatively low overheads can do just that very thing. Also the high overhead cost solicitor hasn't got the specialist in his office to look up the law on many different areas. A divided profession provides this service more cheaply and more efficiently than in any other way.'

The difficulty about this argument is that we have never tried any other way so we have no real basis for comparing costs. If we look at countries with a unified legal profession (such as the United States) we can only consider their costs and expenses which are often negotiated on a different basis from those in this country. For example, contingency fees exist which mean that the lawyer for a claimant is paid from any compensation awarded. The problems with such a system are considered in Chapter Three but it is very hard to say that a divided profession is cheaper or more expensive without looking at every aspect of costing and organisation in other countries. Moreover we do not know what a unified profession in this country would look like. In Chapter Six some modest changes are considered which might improve the present system. It is more realistic to aim for these than for complete fusion which at present looks a very long way off.

In 1985 Robert Alexander QC, an exceptionally energetic Chairman of the Bar, 'emerged' (there are no elections although these are now proposed) and began to modify some of the more criticised of the Bar's practices. He adopted a very open style by giving many press, radio and television interviews and clearly wanted to achieve change but to avoid fusion with solicitors at all costs. He was instrumental in starting a new journal for barristers called *Counsel*, and in 1986 the first annual conference of the Bar was being planned. Some of the articles in the first issue of this journal made odd reading. One of them took a page to describe and even question the strange custom whereby barristers do not shake hands with each other. In another part of the same issue members of the south-east circuit (a largely historical reflection of the division of the country into areas that could be covered in less than one day by horse) were urged to take complaints about accommodation and facilities in courts to the Wine Committee!

Perhaps this kind of quaint organisation and structure is of little significance. But the very need to project a more attractive image of the Bar shows how problematic its position had become. It could no longer rely on assumptions about the necessity for a separate Bar to ensure its survival. In the same issue a leading criminal practitioner and Chairman of the Criminal Bar Association wrote: 'The Bar is and must be an elitist profession. We are not in business to featherbed the inadequate or inefficient among us.' In another passage he captured graphically the dilemma of the Bar – on the one hand an independent profession, on the other, major recipients of public expenditure in the form of fees for criminal legal aid work.

'If the fees negotiations do not produce a satisfactory result, this Government will stand accused of destroying finally the viability of professional criminal practice at the independent Bar.' He does not deal with the dilemma nor, it seems, ask why countries which have salaried defenders and prosecutors represent a threat to liberty. These questions cannot be avoided for long.

The Bar at Work

At another level the services of a barrister are essential. We have already seen that most cases do not come to a full hearing. Either they result in an early judgment for the claimant or there is a settlement because the outcome is too uncertain to risk extensive and expensive litigation. We shall look later at the role of solicitors in promoting settlements. What is also important is the role of the barrister. About ten per cent of the Bar are senior barristers known as 'Queen's Counsel'. This does not mean that they give advice to the Crown, but that they are the successful applicants for 'silk' (they wear silk robes in court). They are chosen by the Lord Chancellor's Department for merit and ability. There is also a concern to see that each specialist area of the practising Bar is fairly represented.

These barristers are in a very special position. They argue important cases. But they also have a wider function. It is their unstated and unnoticed task to set the boundaries of the legal endeavours of lawyers and their clients. That is, they have the role of advising in substantial cases as to whether a particular novel legal argument is likely to be found attractive by the judges. In this they are almost acting as judges (or quasi-judges) themselves. After many years of practice and with their intimate knowledge of the minds of the judiciary they can usually say what the prospects are of a particular argument being successful. This may be seen as a perversion of justice where decisions about whether to bring or abandon a legal action are taken in secret with intuition playing at least some part in the process. But given a divided profession it reflects the reality of the litigation process. Queen's Counsel will have built up their knowledge of the way the judiciary think from various sources. First there is the organisation of the Bar itself. There are four Inns of Court (Inner Temple, Middle Temple, Lincoln's Inn and Grays' Inn). These are autonomous bodies run by 'Benchers' who are judges, Queen's Counsel and a very small number of other barristers. Every aspiring barrister must join an Inn to be called to the Bar and the Inns provide library and social facilities and also own, between them, that small area of London immediately surrounding the Law Courts where about half of the practising Bar has 'chambers'.

The governance of the Bar is, to say the least, complex. Apart from the Inns there is a small central body known as the Senate which has authority to take decisions for the whole Bar, notably in regard to discipline, education and training. There is also a body known as the Bar Council which is representative of the Bar as a whole. Nobody can say with precision which body performs which particular function. There is a bewildering variety of committees, sub-committees and working parties whose authority may derive from an Inn, the Senate or the Bar Council. Given the small size of the Bar it is hardly surprising that the senior judges (in practice chosen exclusively from former members of the Bar) retain a powerful influence over the affairs of the Bar. They constantly meet Queen's Counsel either formally in court or less formally within the Inns or on one or more committees or sub-committees.

Quite apart from this, senior barristers and judges will have known each other for many years because of another organisational aspect of the Bar. Barristers are self-employed, but work in close proximity with other barristers who are organised in sets of chambers. Therefore personal contact between judge and barrister may have begun many years previously.

There is perhaps something too clublike and too restricted about such contacts. But they are the reality of the present system and the semi-judicial function of senior barristers is an unavoidable and necessary part of litigation.

The Judges

The role of the judges themselves is of great importance. Unlike the practice in most of continental Europe and the United States judges do not have a research staff of their own. The necessary research for individual cases is intended to be carried out primarily by the barristers arguing the case. Written argument on points of law is not generally required. This means that when a case raises a point of law the issues will have to be gone into in detail by oral presentation. This is a very slow procedure as it is usual for the relevant passages of previous cases to be read aloud and often in their entirety. A dialogue often develops between judge and barrister whereby the judge puts questions to the barrister of a complex and difficult nature. The barrister is expected to have the facility of replying cogently and convincingly on the spot which is by no means easy. In the Court of Appeal it is now the practice to require skeleton arguments to be prepared and submitted in advance of the hearing. In the House of Lords it has long been necessary for each party to lodge a written 'case' which sets out the legal arguments to be deployed. However, this is rarely referred to at the hearing, is never printed as part of the report of the case and does not seem to do much by way of shortening the oral hearing.

It is a rule of conduct at the Bar that reference should be made to all relevant decisions whether they are helpful or not to the legal argument being advanced. This indicates that the barrister is both a partisan advocate and a 'friend of the court' whose aim is to assist the judge (and presumably to further the interests of justice) by acting almost impartially. There is another, less well perceived consequence of this practice of concentrating all the legal and factual arguments at the final hearing. It tends to prolong the case and to shift the costs of paying for the hearing to the parties to the case.

The Litigation Process – an Example

This point may be seen more clearly if we examine the litigation process at work. To present a claim requires completion of a formal document known as a *writ* in the High Court and a *summons* in the County Court. In simple cases solicitors will draft these documents themselves. In more complex cases a barrister will be instructed to prepare the proceedings in accordance with a traditional style of drafting. For example, suppose that Mrs Smith is driving her car along a main road when Mr Brown pulls out from a side road without taking care to see that his path was clear. A collision occurs and both drivers are injured. It might be possible to use precisely that language with the addition of dates, times and a little more detail to present a claim. Indeed if Mrs Smith decided to act for herself and went to the County Court it would accept a claim written in such a way.

In legal terms the documents look rather different. The events of the accident would be set out in a formal style with the date, location and time included. There will be great emphasis on what Mr Brown is said to have done incorrectly. For example, instead of saying '. . . he drove carelessly . . .' the document will probably say:

'. . . the defendant was negligent in that:
(i) he emerged from a side-road into the path of the plaintiff (claimant) without ensuring that it was safe to do so;
(ii) he failed to ensure that there was any or any sufficient space between his car and that driven by the plaintiff before so emerging;
(iii) he failed to stop, swerve or otherwise avoid the said accident;
(iv) he collided with the car driven by the plaintiff.'

This is repetitive and adds very little to what could be said in simpler continuous prose. It is a form of drafting followed because, it is suggested, it tells the defendant and his or her lawyers precisely what is alleged to have happened and what the defendant is supposed to have done wrong. A similar form of wording is used when the injuries suffered are set out and any loss of earnings is claimed or the cost of repairing damage to vehicles is part of an action. And these are merely simple cases. In a complex commercial case the formal court documents (known as 'pleadings') will run to very many pages.

In a defended case the defence to the claim will be equally formal although the defendant is entitled to enter a general denial and require the plaintiff to prove the case. In some cases the defence may suggest that someone else is to blame and that person may be joined as a 'third party' to the action. For example, following the case above, a defence in a claim for damages resulting from a road traffic accident may suggest that the accident was caused by a defective tyre blowing out and causing the driver to lose control. But it may be hard to show that all control was lost. So the tyre manufacturer might be joined as a third party. In turn that manufacturer might allege that the real problem was caused by the defective fitting of the tyre and the tyre fitting company might be joined as a 'fourth party'.

An able solicitor would have anticipated all these arguments and would have investigated the state of each vehicle. Unfortunately this does not always happen. Either the vehicles are not available for examination, or, if they are, the necessary steps to secure the evidence proving someone is at fault are not taken at an early stage. Michael Joseph, in his recent book on personal injury litigation, *Lawyers Can Seriously Damage Your Health*, argues strongly that solicitors do not perform very well in such cases, although he bases his assertions on a small sample of cases. He claims that solicitors often fail to secure the crucial evidence at the earliest possible stage even though there are court procedures which enable, for example, a damaged tyre to be ordered to be preserved or medical records to be inspected to see whether a case might exist where medical negligence is alleged. One reason for this is that rapid procedures tend to be expensive and it is not always easy to obtain legal aid very speedily. Another, according to Michael Joseph, is the expectation by solicitors that evidence can be left until nearer the hearing. The level of efficiency is hard to measure but it may be the case that the more experienced the solicitors, the more likely it is that the necessary evidence will be gathered at an early stage.

The time element in these pre-trial procedures is also important. Under the rules of procedure laid down by the courts the notional time limits are very short – usually only a matter of days. In practice such periods cannot be adhered to. Papers have to go to and from barristers. Clients have to be consulted and investigations have to occur. A period of months is a more likely time scale within which the formal part of litigation may be conducted. After the pleadings are complete the next step is the exchange of lists of relevant documents. In some cases this will be a very simple process. In complex commercial cases there will be thousands of documents and some large firms now use computers to log and classify the papers they hold. Only after this part of the case is complete (known technically as 'discovery and inspection of documents') can the case be set down for a hearing. In the

County Court one might have to wait for two or three months for a date. In the High Court the delay may be up to one year. It is during this time that negotiations for a settlement are most likely to take place.

In February 1986 the Lord Chancellor issued a consultation paper on personal injury litigation. This proposed radical changes in procedures to reduce the costs and to speed up the process. A speedier timetable would be imposed on the parties and the court would take a closer interest in progress made. Each side would have to make earlier and fuller disclosure of its case. There was broad acceptance of the proposals on their publication and some reform may be expected shortly. What the paper (and the study which led to it) avoids is the broader question: should we retain a fault-based system of personal injury law which, by requiring proof of another person's omission or error, is the main source of delay? Or should we follow the example of New Zealand and adopt a 'no-fault' system at least for injuries resulting from road traffic accidents? This question has been much discussed, but the present government sees some value in the fault-based system as reflecting notions about who deserves compensation and who does not. This shows that, as with most legal issues, the question of reform is essentially political. In a democratic society this should not be surprising.

Other Ways of Resolving Disputes

So far we have restricted our enquiry to formal court procedures. If the system is used properly there is every probability that an individual plaintiff with a good to strong case will be able to bring the claim before a court within a reasonable period. But not all claims can be heard by the courts. Many disputes that arise today are heard by tribunals. And redress via the courts, even where it is available, may have to give way to less formal procedures that bring results but avoid the delay and cost of opposed litigation. Moreover, as we have already seen, most cases that are contested are eventually settled without a formal hearing.

Any picture of the legal system that ignores these features of its operation would be both incomplete and misleading. A much fuller idea of the scope of redress mechanisms available to individuals who claim to have suffered harm can only be obtained by taking a very broad look at the possibility of some form of remedy.

Tribunals

These bodies are more similar to the courts than any other part of the non-formal grievance machinery. A diagram of major tribunals is shown on page 40. They have developed in a somewhat haphazard way and there is nothing very new about them. Each time the state has expanded its welfare and regulatory activities it has recognised that disputes may arise as to how state power has been exercised. There are various possible solutions to this problem. It is conceivable that disputes should be resolved by the ordinary courts. It is equally possible to set up a special type of court or tribunal which is not part of the ordinary court system. Another possibility is to make no special provision and give no right of appeal to the courts. This would tend to leave Ministers or local authorities open to involvement in many individual cases. Yet a further means of resolving disputes is to set up an informal review procedure with little or no legal element contained within its scheme or structure.

All of these methods have been used in the past and continue to be used. But some are more commonly found than others. The ordinary courts have a number of areas of special jurisdiction. We can see this in operation in the field of housing and the related field of public health. Local authorities have wide powers of supervision and control over housing conditions in their area. These powers include the right to serve notices on the owners (usually landlords) of sub-standard properties with a view to improving their condition. If the notice is served under housing legislation the owner of the property can usually appeal to the local County Court against the notice on various grounds. For example, the owner can say that the work specified is not necessary or would be disproportionately expensive given the present value of the house. If, however, the notice is served under public health legislation the appeal goes to the local Magistrates' Court.

By contrast other disputes about housing are dealt with by specialised bodies that are not part of the court system. A tenant who thinks the rent is too high can apply to a Rent Officer for a reduction. The landlord can also apply for an increase every two years. From the Rent Officer there is an appeal to a Rent Assessment Committee. In the employment field a person who is dismissed may bring a claim for unfair dismissal or redundancy compensation before an industrial tribunal.

In the field of social security many disputes arise each year – about 40,000 appeals are brought before local Social Security

MAJOR TRIBUNALS

TRIBUNAL	APPEAL	FURTHER APPEAL
INDUSTRIAL TRIBUNAL	EMPLOYMENT APPEAL TRIBUNAL	COURT OF APPEAL
SOCIAL SECURITY	SOCIAL SECURITY COMMISSIONERS	COURT OF APPEAL
IMMIGRATION ADJUDICATORS	IMMIGRATION APPEAL TRIBUNAL	HIGH COURT
RENT OFFICERS	RENT ASSESSMENT COMMITTEE	HIGH COURT

Appeal Tribunals. There is a possible further appeal to a Social
Security Commissioner. Immigrants whose claims to enter or
remain in this country are rejected by the Home Office can appeal
to an adjudicator with possible further appeal to the Immigration
Appeal Tribunal. A different form of dispute resolution exists in
the area of planning. If the local authority refuses an application
for planning permission an appeal goes to the Department of the
Environment. In practice the appeal is heard by an inspector who
visits the site and who has to weigh up the landowner's wish to
develop as against the local authority's reasons for refusal and
broad government policies relating to planning and land use.

Yet other examples exist. A person who is injured by a criminal has a claim to compensation paid by the state. (In theory a
claim could be made against the criminal but most will have no
money or will not be traceable.) The Criminal Injuries Compensation Board is responsible for assessing claims and paying the
money due.

Tribunals and Courts – why the Difference?

Most writers on the legal system explain the existence of these
special (and specialised) bodies by pointing out that such methods
of resolution are cheaper, speedier and more effective than placing
the matter for hearing before the local courts. There is some truth
in this but the explanation is both incomplete and misleading. It is
incomplete because it takes no account of those instances where
the courts are involved and misleading because it ignores all the
other parallel forms of redress available.

A more complete and sophisticated explanation would point
to other factors at work. First, a decision to exclude the ordinary
courts cuts off a source of work for solicitors and barristers
because, in most cases, legal aid is not available for tribunals. A
more limited form of access to legal advice is available but very
little money is spent on areas such as social security or housing.
(This is known as the 'green form' scheme and is dealt with more
fully on page 82.) And while it is true that the ordinary courts
would not be able to cope with many more areas of jurisdiction
without additional resources, this does not explain why these
resources were and are not made available.

A better explanation for the existence of so many tribunals is
that some disputes are not seen as raising questions of law and are
best left to these bodies because we wish to indicate that normally
accepted judicial standards simply do not apply. It is true that the

courts often have delays in bringing cases to a hearing whereas tribunals do not. There is no complex system of pleadings and (usually) only limited discovery of documents. But these procedures do not exist simply to cause delay although they may well have this effect. They are symbolic of a wish to protect the interests of each party by preventing a case from being heard until each side of the dispute has been fully aired and expressed in writing. Many do not think that a small claim for a social security payment is worthy of such treatment. Perhaps it is not. But it is only since the Royal Commission on Legal Services remarked in 1979 that, for the majority of the population a dispute was far more likely to be heard before a tribunal than before the courts, that tribunals have come to be examined more closely.

That some coherence to this system is needed can be seen from recent developments in tribunal procedures. First, many tribunals now operate under a presidential system. For example, in social security tribunals (which have to deal with the complexities of national insurance and supplementary benefit) there is a president whose task is to monitor the performance of local tribunals all over the country. He has the services of full-time regional chairmen to assist him. In turn they are responsible for the work of part-time chairmen (usually solicitors or barristers) and for the training of the other members of the tribunal. (They are present to reflect the interests of claimants generally.) There has been a great deal of criticism of these tribunals in the past based on their tendency to make moral judgments about the worth or merit of claimants and their inability to follow complex legal issues. The efforts to improve the quality of decision-making are very desirable. But this does not mean that a system that substitutes a tribunal for a court yet does not have any adequate means of ensuring that claimants can get access to advice and, if they wish, representation, is somehow operating to the same standards as the courts at their best.

It is interesting to see that figures for social security tribunals show that representation for the claimant (not necessarily legal representation) dramatically improves the chances of success. What does this say about the nature of decision-making where claimants are not represented? Can the tribunals act themselves as the claimant's representative and require the government to explain and justify its decision in detail? We cannot assume that all unrepresented or absent appellants have recognised that their cases are weak. If the tribunals cannot protect their interests then the claim to informality and greater justice rings very hollow. It is also worth noting that one function of an appeal in social security is to generate an internal DHSS review at a higher level than the original decision maker. This can lead to as many as one third of adverse decisions being altered. What about the cases where there is no appeal?

A slightly different but equally complex comment is often made about industrial tribunals. It is said that they have become legalistic and over technical, making it difficult for claimants to represent themselves and to put their complaint against the employer in simple terms. It is hard to know exactly what this complaint means. If it is that the tribunal has become too like a court then this may be because questions of unfair dismissal and redundancy do raise questions of law which cannot always be answered in a very simple way. The criticism might be better made that inadequate advice and representation facilities are available to protect the interests reflected in the legalistic procedures adopted by the tribunals. If the critics means that there is no need for general principles or procedures and that each case can be decided on its own facts then that would be an invitation to conceal the principles that must inform any decision behind a screen of informality which may only confuse claimants as to their rights. It is also argued that tribunals in, say, social security divert attention from the politics of the issue. The question is not how much is spent on anti-poverty programmes generally but how much this individual is entitled to receive – if anything. Legalising individual cases does not, in fact, appear to limit political activity relating to social security.

The main weakness of tribunals is not that they make bad or unfair decisions but that they may not be capable of modifying the inequality of a system that ensures that the government or, say, an employer can or will always be represented whilst providing no special facilities for claimants other than a vague expectation that the tribunal itself will somehow fill the gap. More information is needed about how well tribunals meet this problem.

Supervision of Tribunals

There is a body known as the Council on Tribunals which was set up following a report by the Franks Committee in 1957. It is a small and little known watchdog with few resources and it can only monitor the work of tribunals in the most general of ways. Its main function is to see that tribunals conform to the criteria of 'openness, fairness and impartiality' identified by the Committee as the necessary attributes of an adequately functioning tribunal system. The problem with these criteria is that they are so vague and general that they are capable of an infinite variety of meanings in the context of the work of any individual tribunal. The annual report of the Council reads in a rather despairing manner as it indicates how meagre its resources are and how government departments rarely comply fully with their obligation to consult the Council on proposals to set up new tribunals or to modify the procedural rules relating to any particular tribunal. The latest report complains that consultation over one proposal had to take place in a matter of days. As the Council is composed almost entirely of part-time members with a small secretariat this is a very reasonable complaint.

Apart from this form of supervision it is possible to appeal to the High Court on a point of law from the decisions of most tribunals.

Other Routes to Justice

What needs to be considered is a broader perspective on grievance mechanisms. In some areas of governmental activity there are well recognised (but entirely unwritten or uncodified) procedures for obtaining a reconsideration or review of an adverse decision. Take some examples. In the field of immigration there is as complex a means of obtaining a review as in almost any other area of governmental decision-making. A person arrives at a port and claims entry as a visitor for a month or two. If that person is a Commonwealth citizen then, in general, no visa is needed so there is no reason to obtain some sort of advance permission to enter from a British official abroad, although such a permission may be obtained on request. If the immigration officer thinks that the individual is not a genuine visitor then entry will be refused. This occurs because in some cases the officer believes that more than a visit is intended and the would-be entrant will seek work. This view may or may not be well founded. There is a right of appeal but the law provides that it can only be exercised from abroad so it will often be of no practical use. The government recognises this because it is a well established convention that the person will not be removed immediately if a Member of Parliament gets in touch with the private secretary of the Home Office Minister who has responsibility for immigration. The individual may then be given 'temporary admission' (which is not a formal recognition of visitor status) although he or she may be detained in the mean-time. The Minister will then consider the file and confirm or overturn the immigration officer's decision. All this takes weeks if not months and, by the end of that time, the would-be entrant may have had the benefit of remaining for the period originally requested. An additional possibility is that judicial review might be available against a wholly misconceived refusal by an immigration officer.

This is only one example of a legal service being provided by an MP. In a recent book called *Grievances, Remedies and the State* Patrick Birkinshaw, a law lecturer, has exhaustively researched such informal methods of obtaining redress for grievances against central and local government. He points out that the growth of judicial review in recent years may become stifled (largely for the reasons suggested in Chapter One) and that the limited rules about standing and the absence of class actions may restrict the growth of this remedy as a means of protecting collective rights and interests. (Class actions are an American phenomenon; they allow all persons affected by a wrong to benefit from the proceed-ings, whether they are a named party or not.) He then points to the existence of many other means of complaining about govern-ment decisions. His list is lengthy. It includes correspondence by MPs with government departments, the likelihood being that a letter to a Minister about a constituent's complaint will receive a reply drafted by a higher official than the one who took the original adverse decision.

Birkinshaw goes on to look at the work of local councillors (particularly in the case of disputes about housing the homeless, the allocation of housing generally and educational matters). He also considers the work of Consumer Councils for nationalised industries and how these will be affected by privatisation, the Police Complaints Board, the BBC and the Independent Broad-casting Authority and agencies such as the Commission for Racial Equality and the Equal Opportunities Commission. It is not possible here to deal in detail with the work of each of these bodies. What is important to notice is that it is largely an arbitrary matter whether there is a right of appeal to the courts, to a tribunal or merely (or perhaps in addition) a right to place a grievance before some other body.

The Ombudsman

Among such other bodies are the institutions of 'ombudsmen'. This is a Swedish word meaning literally 'grievance man'. There is a central government and health service ombudsman (known as the 'Parliamentary Commissioner for Administration') and a number of local government ombudsmen (known collectively as 'the Commission for Local Administration'). Their function is to investigate 'maladministration' which is not defined. In broad terms it excludes an inquiry into the merits of a decision but includes discovering whether there was delay, neglect, misleading advice, rudeness, inadequate explanations given, bias or even corruption. There is a requirement that complaints be presented via an MP or local councillor respectively unless the complaint is that the councillor has not acted properly. Clearly this is a rather lengthy way of challenging adverse decisions but is useful where there is no direct right of appeal and no other channel of complaint has produced a useful result. There is no absolute requirement that central or local government follow the recommendations of a report, but they usually do. In the case of the health service there is no power to question decisions based on 'clinical judgment' but this gap has partly been met by a little known procedure for referring such complaints for an internal review and for an independent review by two consultants.

Given that decisions made by private bodies are also likely to cause disquiet, hardship or even financial loss for individuals it is interesting to note that two large financial groupings – insurance companies and banks – have set up their own ombudsman systems to adjudicate about disputes between individuals and their insurers or bankers. This may include, in the case of banking, awarding financial compensation even though a court action might be a more appropriate way of proceeding. This may be seen as a sensitive response by financial interests to the numerous problems of misunderstandings, difficulties and mistakes that may occur in dealings related to money. Little is known about how these ombudsmen operate in practice and more research may be needed. Political critics of these systems suggest that by conceding individual claims powerful groups in society seek to deny the basic inequality between themselves and their customers. There is also a problem of the independence of such ombudsmen when their costs and salaries are met by the body or interest against which a claim is made.

The key questions in all of these diverse forms of redress for grievances are whether or not there is adequate access to them, whether individuals have an opportunity of presenting their complaints personally if they are not used to preparing a written summary of what they say has gone wrong, and whether their grievances will be met (if they are real) promptly and effectively. At present there is a bewildering variety of procedures available, most of which are (erroneously) not seen as part of the legal system because they lack formality or the involvement of a court. A thorough review and classification of all such remedies would appear to be necessary.

Avoiding the Law and the Courts

Despite these differences, it would be wrong to think that there is a sharp contrast between legal procedures involving court actions and other, more diffuse means of redressing grievances for two reasons. First, the formal mechanism of the law is often bypassed or halted in practice because a case is settled at some stage between the commencement of proceedings and the final hearing. Second, there are strong moves afoot within legal circles to introduce greater informality into judicial proceedings with the aim of reducing costs and also increasing the participation of litigants in their own cases.

Settling Claims

Take the process of settlements first. I will postpone a discussion of the costs of litigation and legal services generally until Chapter Four, but it is the fear of having to meet a large bill for costs that often leads to actions being settled. There are other reasons for reaching a compromise in litigation. Cases take a long time to come to a hearing. There is often uncertainty about the outcome especially in claims for compensation for personal injury. The claimant may be partly at fault and may wish to give up the right to have a judge decide the degree of fault of each party in return for an immediate lump sum. It is generally not possible to settle tribunal claims for social security or other state benefits, however, as the government does not operate in such a manner – either the appeal generates an internal review with the claimant receiving something or it goes to a full hearing.

In cases between an individual and an employer relating to unfair dismissal there will be great pressures to settle. Take the common occurrence of someone in an executive position in a specialised concern dismissed for no stated reason. In theory a good claim for unfair dismissal exists. In practice matters are not so straightforward. The tribunal can only award up to about £8,000 as compensation. It is far from clear what view it will take about the period of time in which the dismissed worker will be expected to find a new job. After that time has gone by no further compensation for loss of pay can be given. The employee has no legal right to a reference but one may be offered as part of the terms of settlement. The tribunal can order reinstatement in the previous job but rarely does so. Consequently, there is every incentive to settle even for a modest sum and then to get on with the effort of finding fresh employment. Indeed the possibility of a settlement is built into the tribunal process because each complaint presented to an industrial tribunal is copied and sent to the Advisory Conciliation and Arbitration Service (ACAS) whose function is to try and promote a settlement before the hearing. There is not (and cannot be) any guarantee that the settlement reached will be fair.

The main problem where solicitors are involved is also whether the settlement recommended to the client is fair. Negotiating is a very skilled area of work yet, as we will see, few solicitors have any training in its techniques and methods. There is some evidence that settlements are often reached in personal injury cases at too low a figure. In negotiating, each side is trying to estimate the strength of its own case and the weaknesses of that of the opponent. The formal process of pleading I referred to earlier is only an approximate indicator of what the evidence behind the claim or defence might be. Success in negotiating depends upon the experience of the solicitor, the skill of the defendant's representative (usually an insurance company claims manager) and the degree of knowledge each party has as to current levels of damages awards for injury, including uncertain forms of loss such as pain and suffering, inability to lead a normal life and the difficulties of assessing the medical prognosis. Also relevant is whether the solicitor has consulted a barrister specialising in such cases and whether the solicitor and the client have the resources, time and patience to reject what may be too low an initial offer. It will be seen that the actual strength or weakness of the case may be less important than the perception by either party of such strength. Every piece of uncertainty and risk as to the eventual outcome is a powerful weapon in the hands of an insurance company or other defendant. No means exist for ensuring that the settlement is a fair and reasonable balance between competing claims. In only one case does the court have any role to play. That is where an action is settled on behalf of a minor – a person under eighteen. Here it is necessary to show to the court that the settlement is a fair one and a full inquiry is undertaken to ensure that this is so.

Informal Justice

In addition to the various devices and institutions discussed above for diverting claims from the courts, there are suggestions that our normal court procedures should become more informal.

It is very common to hear criticisms of and even attacks upon the expansion of legal rights and remedies. There are many examples of this. The breach of the monopoly of solicitors over conveyancing is one. Another is the wish to introduce informal mediation procedures in the divorce courts which are intended to reduce the tension and bitterness often characteristic of legal intervention in disputes over child custody and the division of property. The courts are also said to be too busy and there is too much litigation. The prisons are overcrowded and there are calls for decriminalisation of motoring offences. Some private be-haviour is seen as not worthy of legal control – drug use (at least of 'soft' drugs) is one example. Outside the legal sphere we can see other examples. There are calls to dismantle other institutions such as mental hospitals and to provide instead care in the com-munity.

Not all of these developments are directly related to each other. There is as much evidence of a desire to give greater powers to the police as there is of a desire to introduce community policing and greater local control over police activities. But if we focus upon two active areas of experiment and change in legal proce-dures we can see both benefits and detriments within the move to greater informalism.

Consumers and the Law

First, let us consider consumer complaints. There is a far greater awareness today of the rights of consumers in relation to shoddy goods and poor quality services. This consciousness of grievances and of the possibility of a remedy was once, perhaps, limited to the middle classes and highly paid employees but it has now become widespread. Radio and television programmes have effectively helped to spread the word that consumers are not powerless. The Consumers' Association, with its high circulation *Which?* magazine, has expanded its influence and is a recognised pressure group in the political arena. Parallel with this there have been developments in the actual delivery of consumer rights. In the County Court there is a 'small claims' procedure where the amount in dispute is less than £500. Such cases are referred to arbitration before the registrar. The formal rules of evidence are waived and, above all, no legal costs can be recovered, so this has the makings of a speedy and cheap procedure for reducing the fear and expense of litigation. Such procedures are not limited to the County Court. For six years in the mid-seventies a number of experimental small claims procedures were set up in Westminster with the aid of a grant from the Nuffield Foundation. There was a similar scheme in operation in Manchester. Each scheme was essentially an arbitration procedure where the consumer and the seller or provider of services both agreed to present their claims and defences to a lawyer. There was a simple written statement by both parties and an arbitrator – usually a local solicitor – would consider the case and hear both sides in an informal manner. There would also be an inspection of the item or services in dispute. In general, once persuaded to accept the authority, of the system the party found to be in the wrong would accept the arbitrator's decision. As Tony Conway, the administrator of the scheme, put it:

'. . . without the mysticism, without the magic attached to the law, without the wigs, the gowns, the courts, the standing up, the sitting down, people still accepted what was happening . . . Sometimes we used their own front rooms if a settee was involved. If there was a boundary dispute we'd hold it in the back garden. So we'd take the court to the people, so to speak.'

The scheme involved the use of a panel of experts who would inspect the television or settee or whatever was being argued about. This avoided the problems which arise in the ordinary courts (even in the small claims procedures in the County Court) where each side has an expert witness and the court has to decide between them. The scheme came to an end because the finances available to run the administration and keep records simply ran out. However, its impact has spread to other areas of consumer grievances. A number of trade associations have been persuaded to establish arbitration schemes for remedying consumer grievances. Some examples are the scheme set up by the Association of British Travel Agents to deal with complaints about package holidays and a similar scheme set up by the Motor Agents' Association for complaints about poor quality work by garages.

What these systems have in common is that they are sponsored by the Office of Fair Trading which has, as one of its functions, the protection of consumers. The usual pattern is to encourage the trade association to step in when a dispute arises, initially as a conciliator. If this fails then the complaint can go forward to a cheap and simple arbitration with an independent arbitrator appointed by the Institute of Arbitrators. The trade association basis of these schemes has the further advantage that failure to meet an award will result in expulsion from the association. In addition, an arbitration award can be enforced through the ordinary courts.

The existence of the insurance and banking ombudsmen has already been referred to. Sir Gordon Borrie, Director-General of Fair Trading, welcomes such further means of meeting grievances as 'a very useful alternative . . . let's have many different forms of settling disputes'. Of course, such schemes are of little use if the trader does not belong to the trade association. The only remedy then would be an ordinary action in the County Court. A further possibility in difficult cases is a complaint to the local Trading Standards Officer who can bring a criminal prosecution under, for example, the Trade Descriptions Acts. These enable Magistrates' Courts to impose fines for misleading consumers as to the quality or state of goods and can also award compensation for breaches of the criminal law.

In general, the statistics show that both small claims procedures, arbitrations and the short-lived voluntary schemes produced a successful outcome for claimants. There was some evidence from a survey conducted by the National Consumer Council to show that some courts were more helpful to claimants than others and some registrars found it difficult to modify their traditional and formal ways. Many problems were found in relation to the giving of expert evidence because, unlike the voluntary schemes, the courts expect the parties to bring forward the evidence and to prove or disprove the claim without asking the court to find and appoint an expert. Also it is not clear how far all types of people can make full use of these procedures as opposed to the articulate and capable middle-class consumer. In this respect the voluntary procedures were probably more successful because they moved away from adversarial procedures to an investigative form of hearing – a kind of informal inquiry. What is essential in any type of scheme is that it should be made well known to the general public and there is some evidence that the trade association arbitrations are not familiar to most consumers. Moreover each scheme has different procedures and varying fees have to be paid to initiate a claim.

A Critique of Small Claims Procedures

Three critiques have been developed of the overall methods of enforcing small claims. The first points to the need to move to genuinely participatory, inquisitorial procedures which make the position of the parties equal by giving the decision-maker wide powers to investigate and decide. The formal processes of justice offer procedural safeguards at least to the well advised and well represented claimant. But, because formal litigation tends to favour the 'repeat players' (to use an American description of companies who often sue) against the 'one shotter' (the consumer), there is a need to limit formality in order to produce greater access to justice without legal assistance. The solution is seen (notably by the National Consumer Council) to be a modification of court procedures to introduce more informality and an investigative role for the Registrar. This approach seeks to ensure that the wealth of law designed to protect the consumer is not pushed into the background in favour of some vague notion of what is fair and just in any given case. As yet, however, no major changes to court procedure have been introduced.

The second proposal is much more radical. It suggests that the County Courts have become a routine system for processing debt recovery claims with little or no inquiry into the merits and worth of individual cases. Indeed it is creditors who now widely use small claims procedures. Some researchers have argued that it should no longer be possible for debt claims (below an unspecified figure) to be enforced. This would ensure that credit was not given so easily and reliance was placed on most people's wish to pay their way. To produce better justice for claimants it is argued that more flexible schemes are needed with access to an instant form of justice dispensed by a mobile team of young, able and consumer-oriented judges who can visit the complainant's home and reach a decision on the spot. Such proposals may seem far-fetched but are interesting for their novelty. They are unlikely to be adopted and, in any event, are incomplete because there is no logic in looking at one aspect of the contact between individuals and the legal system without taking account of other similar contacts such as tribunals which were discussed above.

A third critique is less a proposal for more simplicity than an attack on the very notion of expanding formal justice. Writing from an American and a Marxist perspective a team of legal academics and practitioners have produced a recent book entitled *The Politics of Informal Justice* (Academic Press, 1982). Richard Abel, a law professor and radical political thinker, suggests that informal complaint mechanisms for consumers distract attention from the fundamental conflict between the owners of capital and the rest of society. Informal justice, he says, mediates conflict, dampens down the demands of consumers and so 'cools out' disgruntled claimants. Moreover he argues that all legal institutions individualise conflicts in society and so steer grievances into acceptable channels. By concentrating on procedures and not on more basic political grievances the power of capital is made to appear equal to that of the poor or, at least, not well-off claimant. He also claims that arbitration and other small claims procedures are invariably imposed by the state and do not arise from any popular demand for informal justice. If the courts represent an ideal of 'due process of law' (to borrow a phrase from the United States Constitution) why should legal representation and normal court procedures be denied on grounds of cost or from a desire to speed up the legal process? He further points out that small claims procedures are often used by creditors against debtors rather than by consumers.

This is an interesting attack, not only on informalism but on the whole legal process. The problem with it is that aggrieved individuals do not always want to fight a political battle against the form of society that exists. Indeed they may have no fundamental quarrel with the social order. Given that society is organised in the way that it is and that the world may not be a perfect place there is a need to devise systems of meeting small claims. Certainly, there is an equal need to ensure that the disadvantaged can make effective use of such procedures and not leave unfair advantage in the hands of the large organisations. To enforce consumer rights may not bring about a fundamental reversal of status by consumers and the 'poor' but it will at least improve material conditions for some individuals.

Mediation and Conciliation

A final form of alternative legal procedure which is under constant discussion is the possibility of mediation and conciliation in divorce. Such schemes take many forms but their essential feature is a wish to find a humane, civilised and harmonious way of resolving problems of family breakdown, notably in the areas of financial provision and care for children. The formal legal process can be expensive, and is often said to generate profits for lawyers but pain for their clients. To reduce the level of conflict can only, it is argued, help the parties to reshape their lives and avoid the adverse effects on the children of some of the traumas involved. Emotional and psychological harm might be limited by reshaping the procedures to bring about a resolution of conflict that is less concerned with legal rights than with what is best for the family.

Such schemes may take the form of conciliation as part of the formal process of divorce or as an additional possibility offered by social workers and other counsellors outside formal court procedures. Solicitors might be excluded from the process as incapable of offering anything but an increase in animosity and bitterness. The emotional, social, legal and practical aspects of the family breakdown can all be dealt with in an informal way. Moreover as most disputes are settled outside court, mediation and conciliation schemes may be seen as an adjunct and rationalisation of what already occurs. Wrapped up in these proposals is a move for reform which would bring under one umbrella the various powers to terminate marriages, make financial orders, provide for children and deal with all other legal aspects of the family. This is the proposal for a 'Family Court' which would take over all the powers at present exercised by Magistrates' Courts, the County Court and the High Court.

At first sight there is everything to be said for these reforms. They might reduce bitterness and help reduce conflict. But a critique of such proposals has been developed by feminists. They argue that an important motivation in such plans is the wish to reduce expenditure on legal aid. They also suggest that women may be disadvantaged in several ways. As a group that is already dominated by men they lack equality in informal procedures. There is no guarantee that a mediator or conciliator will not bring values which are detrimental to women into the negotiations. The power relationship within the family is not subject to the public inquiry of formal justice and established court procedure.

Anne Bottomley, writing in *Women in Law* (Routledge &

Kegan Paul, 1985) edited by Julia Brophy and Carol Smart, argues that formal justice offers more to women than informal conciliation. She identifies three advantages:

> . . . substantive rights, frail as these might be; procedural safeguards (rules about what counts as evidence and rights of appeal, for example); lawyers who can reduce the power imbalance between the parties.'

She goes on to argue that:

> 'Informality, conciliation and an inquisitorial mode of justice . . . offers less protection to weaker or more vulnerable parties and particularly for those who do not conform to prevailing social values.'

This is, of course, only one view. Leaving aside the question of costs there is a great deal of hostility inherent in matrimonial procedures and some reduction of such bitterness might be obtained without a wholesale surrender of women's rights. It has to be recognised that conciliation is on the political agenda but that the dangers of allowing welfare agencies or unprotected and ill-advised individuals to abandon their rights are real and substantial. Divorce is becoming normal and is not seen as a deviant form of behaviour. The rights of men, women and children have to be respected within our procedures for dissolving marriages and resolving related disputes. Indeed it is the respect for individual rights that should motivate all efforts to reform legal processes. Only in this way will procedures emerge that are equitable, accessible and comprehensible.

CHAPTER
3

THE TRAINING OF LAWYERS

For the moment let us accept that law and the legal system has become too pervasive, too problematic, yet too important to our lives to imagine that we can leave its operation to individuals pursuing their own rights. We have already seen that there are pitfalls and dangers inherent in adopting systems of informal justice that assume that the services of lawyers can or should be dispensed with. It then becomes important to ask how lawyers are educated and trained, how they acquire (if they do at all) the skills they need to serve their clients' interests and whether non-lawyers could perform some of the tasks at present reserved to qualified barristers or solicitors.

To become a lawyer is an ambition held by many. As higher education has expanded – despite the fact it is at present going through a phase of 'no growth' and cutbacks – the opportunities for studying at degree level have multiplied. Traditionally entry into the legal profession was not restricted to graduates, let alone graduates in law. School-leavers could study either for the Bar or for the solicitors' examinations for a period of years. They combined this with practical work in lawyers' offices or chambers. While the profession remained static in numbers the majority of entrants followed this route. Invariably they required financial support from their families to complete the academic stage of their transformation into lawyers. This meant that the profession was dominated by the well-off. While the services of lawyers were restricted to dealings in property and the prosecution or defence of criminal charges, this seemed to pose no problems. It was a combination of events that brought significant change to both the profession and the methods of entry and training which opened the gate to legal practice.

Changing the Professions Profile: Legal Education

The starting point for change was the growth of owner-occupation after the end of the last war. Governments of all parties since then have encouraged people to become home owners. As more money was put into housing so prices rose. The demand for the services of lawyers was strengthened because the complexities of English land law effectively prevented house purchase from being as simple as the acquisition of other consumer assets. Solicitors were needed to act in conveyancing transactions. There was also an expanding demand for lawyers to undertake commercial work. Increase in investment by individuals in insurance policies, unit trusts and pension arrangements offered by private companies all contributed to further demands for legal work. At the same time the opportunities for qualifying as a lawyer were increasing. More places were available in universities and polytechnics for the study of law at degree level. It was never essential to have a law degree but the complexity of modern law did tend to make graduate entry to the profession more common. At the same time more public money was being spent on legal services, notably on criminal legal aid. This also increased the demand for legal services at the Bar.

By the mid-seventies graduates had virtually replaced school-leavers as the normal route to qualification as a lawyer. And most of these graduates had a degree in law – a very modern development. Until the middle of the nineteenth century very little law was taught in universities. Law was seen as a vocational subject and hardly fit for study outside schools provided by the profession. Quite why this should have been so while medicine was regarded as a proper subject for study at a school attached to a university, has never been clear. But it had one vital consequence. The length of almost all law degree courses has traditionally been three years. The universities have played no formal part in the vocational training of lawyers after graduation and it has consequently not attracted mandatory grants. This has meant that access to private means or, at least, a willingness to undergo some financial hardship has been essential for the would-be practitioner. The social composition of entrants to the profession has therefore hardly broadened. In addition admission to law schools generally requires high Advanced Level GCE grades.

Currently there are about 4,500 graduates in law each year. Not all intend to practise law. Many simply chose to study law because they believed it would equip them as well as any other degree course for future employment. Most who do wish to practise intend to become solicitors for whom there continues to be a high demand. As will be seen, becoming a barrister is more problematic and only attracts a minority of law graduates.

Teaching the Law

There has always been a constant tension within law departments between the clearly observable fact that many students wish to qualify as lawyers, and the need to make law a respectable subject for purely academic study. Earlier this century the problem was solved by placing the emphasis in law degrees on the philosophy of law (usually called jurisprudence), Roman law and those parts of English law which have largely been judge-made. The most usual topic to be followed was the law of contract which forms the basis of all commercial transactions from the smallest consumer purchase to a vast multi-national agreement to build aircraft or ships. This was followed by the law of tort (from the French word for 'wrong') which deals with civil wrongs that are not simply breaches of contract, such as claims for compensation, for personal injury or harm done to property. Land law (an extremely complex subject), constitutional and administrative law (law dealing with government and administration of the country) and the law of trusts (mechanisms for holding and maintaining private wealth), also formed part of the syllabus. Indeed to be recognised for professional purposes a law degree must contain these 'core' subjects although, in practice, there is a considerable amount of discretion as to how they are taught and whether the whole topic is covered.

The emphasis was on expounding legal doctrine and creating, from a mass of case law, coherent statements of the principles in each given topic. Textbooks of ever increasing length were published and the law schools saw themselves as mainly concerned with a study of the rules of law. In many instances it is not possible to state these rules with any degree of precision so, as more cases are decided which refine and reshape the principles, there is more material to study and more law for textbook writers to work into new editions of their books. It took time to introduce other topics into the syllabus. More modern areas of law such as taxation, employment law, company law and social security law took rather longer to come into the scope of law degrees, mainly because they were (and are) primarily based on statute law and, in consequence, are not part of the tradition of 'common law' that lawyers most easily recognise as their own familiar world. It is something of a caricature, but many law courses do partake of a detailed study of a decision of the House of Lords in, say, *Humpty Dumpty* v. *Jack the Beanstalk* which will then be contrasted with a later decision of the House in, say, *Peter Pan* v. *Mother Goose*. The differences will be analysed, the similarities expounded and a comprehensive critique of the reasoning in each case will be made. This is likely to be repeated in every other topic throughout the three years of study. Such an approach is often termed 'learning black letter law'.

This dry and pedantic approach has been based on the inherent view that all that is worth knowing about the law is the content of its rules. This type of study is very demanding but limited. More recently other views have prevailed at least in some law schools. There are some which want to examine not only the rules of law but their social, historical, political and economic origins, and values embodied within the law itself. This approach also represents an assertion that law is a valuable form of study in its own right irrespective of a student's career intentions, and is sometimes called 'studying law in context'. Whatever the precise approach adopted (and it will vary not only from one law school to another but also between one course and another within the same law school) the academic study of law will rarely involve contact with legal practitioners. Some universities and polytechnics are introducing 'clinical' courses. These involve both studying the law in the books and observing its practical application in the setting of a local law centre or possibly an advice centre directly linked to the law school. The rationale for this approach is not merely that practical and theoretical law complement each other or even that it is important to train future lawyers in this way. Rather it is the idea that legal rules can best be understood by observing their operation in practice.

Training for Solicitors

Law students must make up their minds very early on in a degree course whether they intend to become solicitors. The reasons for this are about as poor as reasons can be. Because the difference in the roles of solicitor and barrister are said to be so great, there is no common post-graduate training and students must book their places on the one-year solicitors' course well before they take their finals. The consequences of this system have scarcely been thought out, nor has any research been done to see whether there is truly such a difference in the work they will eventually do which justifies the need for separate training. In the case of budding solicitors the course is provided by the College of Law (which has a more or less formal relationship with the Law Society) at three branches or at eight polytechnics. Local authority grants for this are, unfortunately, discretionary only. This one year is a very demanding period and is designed to build on theoretical knowledge learned during the academic stage. It prepares students for an examination in some eight areas which are not grouped around academic concepts such as 'property' or 'contract'. Instead they are based on practical classifications such as 'the solicitor and the private client' (this might involve taxation, wills, trusts) or 'the solicitor and the business client' (companies, employment law, some insolvency law). Conveyancing and civil and criminal litigation are examined separately. The emphasis is on the ability to work through a bundle of complex papers which simulate a real problem and then to offer advice in writing, draft a document (a will or some other technical paper) or prepare a letter. Success enables the student to enter the world of practice as an 'articled clerk' (so called because the document evidencing the arrangement is called 'articles of clerkship').

The aim of articles is to gain practical experience in at least three areas of a solicitor's work. The clerk is paid, the salary being at least that of a recommendation made by the Law Society (which governs all aspects of the work of a solicitor), unless for some special reason this is waived. Such a salary will barely be sufficient to live on and many clerks have to depend on their parents for support. Articles last for two years. Inevitably their quality will vary enormously. Large prestigious London firms will try to attract the best qualified students. They will often recruit direct from universities and most would not bother to approach polytechnic law schools. There is no formal system of either employing articled clerks or enabling them to be employed. Social and family links with firms tend to be important although an informal register of solicitors wishing to take clerks is maintained and published by university careers departments.

There is then, plenty of formal training in the law itself and in its practical application. Indeed there is probably too much as the law changes rapidly and the solicitor, unless working in a very specialised field needs a sound knowledge of principles and the ability to look up more obscure or more complex points of detail. What are not formally taught at all are the skills which are needed for professional practice. Practising lawyers often claim that such skills as advocacy (some solicitors at least are advocates), negotiating, interviewing clients and such matters as writing effective letters or drafting legal documents can only be learnt by practice, are unteachable and of a mysterious nature understood by very few. No evidence for such an assertion has ever been gathered. As Professor Twining (a legal theorist but one of the pioneers of the 'law in context' movement) put it:

> 'We have too little theory about practical training rather than too much . . . It's not just lawyers but almost everyone who in their practical affairs has to ask questions, diagnose problems, evaluate evidence, interpret, create and manipulate rules, negotiate, use and abuse statistics, construct and criticise arguments and so on. None of these are a lawyer's monopoly.'

If there is anything peculiar about a lawyer's skills it is that they are often used in special ways, with complex legal materials and in a context of dealing with facts (that may or may not be disputed) and with people – including all the emotions that individuals bring with them into a lawyer's room. But we know little about what all this means in educational terms.

Reforming Legal Education

In 1971 a committee looked into the question of legal education. It was chaired, inevitably perhaps, by a High Court judge, Sir Roger Ormrod. He had a far-sighted vision of what legal education entailed and he envisaged the practical stage of a solicitor's training being carried out not by an apprenticeship system (although he recognised that, if the firm was a good one, the training would be very valuable), but by full-time intensive training in the skills of a lawyer. This was intended to replace both articles and the professional final examination. A visionary model of such a form of training would involve a course run by educational experts and those skilled in professional training, as well as lawyers. But there would be difficulties, notably the assessment of such skills, the development of the course as experience of its problems grew and the relationship between course content and changes occurring in the rules of substantive law and court procedure. Interestingly, in both Scotland and, to a greater degree, in Northern Ireland, skills courses of this type do exist. Nobody has yet put forward a justification for having three different methods of legal training in one state. That the law of each of these parts of the state is different does not seem to be any reason for differences of education.

It is probably the question of cost that made such a system inappropriate in England and Wales. A one-year practical course – perhaps it would have to be longer – would have to be financed either by the government, out of general taxation or by the profession with a levy raised on each practitioner's profits. Neither potential paymaster has shown any inclination to find the money required. So the old system continues with haphazard chances of obtaining a good training. The Royal Commission on Legal Services wanted to see a full review of the efficiency of articles in 1983 and, if this proved that articles were not working well, a new system of vocational training was to be established. Nothing has been done to carry out such a review.

An important innovation in 1985 has been the introduction of a requirement for compulsory continuing education for solicitors. At this stage it is only newly qualified solicitors who have to attend. They must acquire so many 'points' within three years of admission, made up from any number of courses with a compulsory core of accounts and professional practice. This is an interesting and worthwhile development but it seems to put too much emphasis on legal topics not covered in the course leading to the finals, with little or no attention being given to the skills of actually being a lawyer. No doubt this will come in time but it would be more than welcome now.

Education and Training for the Bar

Training for the Bar is somewhat different in nature. There is only one course and this is taught by the Council of Legal Education in London. The teaching is carried out in an overcrowded building but the Bar has always declined to allow any other institution to offer such a course. (A new building is to be opened within the next two years.) The period of study is one year, the focus being upon the abilities needed by a barrister in practice. There are papers on the law of evidence, civil and criminal procedure and the ability to apply legal knowledge in a practical way. These skills are not, however, tested orally (as in a simulated court hearing) but only on paper. It is also necessary to follow a related but separate course of practical exercises in which advocacy techniques are studied and use is made of video cameras to improve style and performance. These exercises are not separately examined. The final examination used to have the reputation of being rather easy but it has become more difficult in recent years. As with the would-be solicitor, a local authority grant for the course is discretionary only.

In addition to following the course, would-be barristers must munch their way through a series of dinners at one of the Inns of Court, which they are required to join. If this sounds absurd, it is because it is absurd. It is justified as a means of introducing aspiring barristers to more senior members of the Inn but there is no guarantee that this happens in practice. The Bar would probably like to abandon the requirement but has not yet had the boldness to do so. It dates from the time that students lived in the Inns and participated in a collegiate life. It serves little or no useful purpose today and nothing would be lost by abandoning it. Were it not for students dining, the Inns would probably not provide any facilities for senior members in the evenings during legal terms so the apparent need for these may be the explanation for the longevity of the institution.

Passing the examinations is followed by a period of apprenticeship known as 'pupillage'. Unlike the articled clerk, the trainee barrister only has to be apprenticed for one year and, after the first six months of that year, can appear in court and earn some money. No payment at all is made during the first six months. What is more, finding a pupillage in the first place is often as difficult as finding a firm to take on an articled clerk. In recent years the Inns have set up pupillage schemes and some chambers of barristers offer scholarships to well qualified applicants. But these systems do not always work well and there have long been complaints that women and members of ethnic minorities find it very difficult to obtain a pupillage. The Bar is at last taking these complaints seriously and has tried to ensure that the discrimination that undoubtedly existed is removed. But how exactly it can do this is not clear. Six months without an income is perhaps not a long period but it assumes parental support. It is quite impossible to justify the need for a trainee to be reliant on the support of others. A small levy on all barristers would raise funds to pay all pupils a reasonable sum. The Bar will surely come to see this soon.

Pupillage, although short, is a very intensive period of learning. It involves reading all the papers sent to the barrister to whom the trainee is a pupil, attending all the barrister's cases in court and also attending the formal 'conferences' with solicitors and their clients which, incidentally, are almost always held in the barrister's chambers and not in the solicitor's office. There will also be an opportunity to read written opinions on cases drawn up by the barrister and a chance to draft these as well as formal pleadings in court cases. As with the articled clerk, the quality of training will depend on the conscientiousness of the barrister, the level of his or her practice and, it must be said, the ability of the pupil. The Royal Commission on Legal Services point to these possible weaknesses in its report in 1979, but apart from endorsing principles of good pupillage practice laid down by the Bar itself, it did not recommend any change to the system. Some training on the job is essential but a lack of any effective control over standards for both articled clerks and pupils is worrying. The Bar has no proposals at present to introduce continuing education for barristers.

Non-Law Graduates

Graduates in subjects other than law can qualify either as solicitors or barristers by following a one-year course in the six 'core' subjects followed by the usual routes to the profession described above. Again there is no obligation on local authorities to give a grant for the one-year course and many do not. As yet there is only a very limited form of part-time study available for this course. Indeed part-time legal education at degree level is relatively undeveloped with only a scattering of courses across the country almost entirely offered by polytechnics. These courses are very popular. Quite a few police officers follow them, hoping to become lawyers when they retire after twenty or twenty-five years' service. They are also attractive to anyone who has missed the chance of degree level education at eighteen. In 1985 it looked as if cutbacks in expenditure in the polytechnic sector would adversely affect both the numbers who could take such courses and the quality of library and teaching provision available. They would also affect the quality of full-time courses available in this sector and possibly the nature of the special courses for the Law Society Final Examination.

In the United States and Canada, law can only be studied at post-graduate level. This means that the overall training period is rather longer and lawyers there are older on qualifying. As there is no prospect of a move in the United Kingdom to such a form of training I will leave aside further comparisons.

Training for Judges

The selection and training of two further groups of practising lawyers need separate treatment. First there are the judges. We have to be careful about definitions here. We might include only judges in the High Court and County Court and Crown Court. (The latter are known collectively as 'circuit judges'.) But this would be misleading for two reasons, First we must also consider the growing group of lawyers, mainly barristers but some solicitors, who sit as part-time judges. These are called recorders and are experienced lawyers in their late thirties and upwards who sit as fully fledged part-time criminal judges on moderately serious cases. They would usually do this for about thirty days each year. In addition a recent innovation is to appoint lawyers as assistant recorders for a three year probationary period before being appointed full recorders. The present Lord Chancellor, Lord Hailsham, has a preference for part-time appointments for all potential members of the judiciary both to see whether they can do the job and also as a form of in-service training.

As well as full- and part-time judges in the courts there are the personnel who staff the complex range of tribunals. They are mainly part-time chairmen and chairwomen who are either practising solicitors or barristers. Some tribunals have full-time chairmen but the more usual pattern is to rely on part-timers. There is a small but growing body of lawyers who occupy most of their time with more than one tribunal appointment. The training given to such lawyers varies but the usual approach today is to arrange for a short course introducing the work of the particular tribunal and for the appointee to sit in for a week or so with an experienced chairman.

Little or no training is given to civil law judges. In the case of criminal judges a Judicial Studies Board was established some years ago to ensure that some training in sentencing and in instructing a jury is given. Sentencing arouses a great deal of public interest (although the full facts of a case heard over many days are rarely reported) and one of the aims of the Board is to achieve consistency by different judges. The Board is careful to avoid the word 'training' in its reports, as this might be taken to imply that there is some threat to judicial independence. This is why the term 'studies' was adopted. There is still some tension between those who see the possibility of training judges as important and those who believe that the adherence to any 'official' line would be detrimental to the exercising of judicial discretion in sentencing. In practice the course in sentencing is run by senior judges and academics interested in criminology. There are visits to prisons and talks by probation officers. There is no sign that the wish of the Home Office to reduce the prison population is transmitted to judges as any kind of direction to avoid custodial sentences. Moreover if, as happens, lay magistrates have to undergo intensive training, it is strange to think that exposure to years of practice is enough by itself to prepare a person to sit as a judge. The tradition is strongly in favour of leaving judges to their own devices, or expecting them to raise problems with more senior members of the judiciary. This is in sharp contrast to the system in some other European countries where judges are not drawn from the ranks of practitioners and undergo separate training from a young age. They do not seem to be any less independent of the state as a result.

Indeed it is sometimes forgotten that judges are paid by the state. Although their constitutional independence is protected and higher judges cannot be removed except by Parliament after a clear case of misconduct, there are no formal procedures laid down for their appointment. Lower judges may be dismissed more summarily. In 1983 a circuit judge was dismissed after he had been fined £2,000 on a charge of smuggling whisky and cigarettes. Other judges have not been dismissed after convictions of drink-driving offences.

Appointing Judges

It is often hard to know why a certain individual was promoted to an appellate court in preference to another. Perhaps the process of judicial appointments needs to be opened up. Why are only minor judicial posts advertised, leaving 'soundings' and the Lord Chancellor's intelligence network to collect information on those who aspire to more senior office? It is true that the range of appointees is narrow given a reluctance to look outside the Bar for the majority of posts, so it is usually said that enough information can be gathered without the need for formal applications. It seems that political opinions are not taken into account when appointing judges although, as Professor Griffith puts it: 'A man or woman whose social or personal habits are unconventional or uncertain is not likely to be risked.' Griffith also points out that higher judges tend to be predominantly male and to have been educated mainly at public schools and at Oxford or Cambridge universities. This will change as more women enter the Bar and as the social background of lawyers begins to reflect a broader spectrum of society.

The main obstacle to significant change is the low rate of earnings for the first few years of practice at the Bar. Another special feature of the judiciary is that appointments do not come until late in career terms – around the age of fifty would be normal. This means that judges are required to sit until aged seventy-two (in some cases, seventy-five) which is perhaps very old to be dealing with the problems of a changing world. It becomes all the more problematic when judges have to deal with diverse aspects of modern law which are often controversial, such as race relations, trade union powers, government decision-making and government secrecy. It is necessary to know that judges are incorruptible and that this quality together with independence of thought characterises their values and activities. Against this there is the narrow social group from which they come and the very wide powers they have to shape and interpret the law. It is important, however, not to overstate their significance. It must be remembered that a vast array of lesser tribunals (and other forms of obtaining redress) are making far more decisions than the judiciary and a much wider spread of social background (and, no doubt, of ability) can be found in these bodies.

There is a curious convention which prevents judges from giving interviews to the media. It has no strict legal basis but was apparently created in the 1950s. It is designed to protect judges from having to explain their decisions and from disclosing their individual social or political views. By 1985 it had come under attack as a form of undesirable censorship. Its most curious feature was that, in the close circles in which judges and senior barristers move (including contact with some legal academics) it was usually well known whether Judge X supports the Conservative party or Judge Y the Labour party. Moreover in such a closed world judges regularly explain and discuss their decisions. It seems that what is known to a few must not be told to many – a reflection of the secrecy inherent in much of public life.

Criminal Justice and Magistrates

Although this book has mainly looked at civil law and civil justice it is worth saying something about those who administer criminal justice. The vast majority of criminal cases are heard by magistrates. As we have seen the great majority of these are not legally qualified. Their appointment was for many years shrouded in mystery. Even today the system of appointment is not well known. The Lord Chancellor is nominally responsible for ensuring that there are sufficient numbers of magistrates. Because of retirements and a general desire to appoint younger magistrates there is a continual need for new appointments to be made. As no payment (other than expenses) is provided there are no financial implications to worry the Treasury. But as a central institution within the administration of justice it is important not only that people should know how magistrates are selected but also that the process should ensure that those appointed are representative both of society as a whole and of the local community. The system is essentially one administered locally. There are Advisory Committees in each county and metropolitan area (the abolition of this tier of local government will not affect the existence of the committees). The work of interviewing candidates and recommending them for appointment is done by sub-committees. Most of the members of both committees are serving or retired magistrates. But their identity is kept secret in order to prevent pressure being put on such persons by candidates or their supporters. It is possible for applicants to approach the secretary of the local committee whose identity is made public. Some organisations, such as political parties and trade unions, will put forward names and some individuals will be proposed by existing magistrates.

The main aim of the selection process is to find suitable candidates and to preserve a balance on the Bench (as magistrates are often known collectively). By 'balance' the Lord Chancellor's Department means a broad cross-section of political and social views. It is therefore necessary to ask candidates to state political opinions and to ensure, as far as possible, that a broad spread of local society is represented in terms of class and race. This ideal is called 'popular justice' by Michael King and Colin May in their recent book on the selection of black magistrates (*Black Magistrates*: Cobden Trust, 1985). They argue that it is important for defendants in the criminal process to be judged by their peers, by people with similar backgrounds, values, attitudes, and who can understand their way of life. They go on to point out that being a magistrate today requires more than being a juror as it includes deciding difficult issues of sentencing, child care and bail.

Opposed to this view is the consideration of expertise and the ability to weigh up evidence. This, King and May term 'professionalism'. They show that if the emphasis is placed on this approach then those appointed will be selected on the basis of being able to benefit from training and on their ability to act in a detached manner. Whichever of these views prevails (and there is a constant tension between them), they also show that there is great cause for concern that members of ethnic minorities rarely come forward for appointment and are rarely appointed. The reasons for this are complex but there is a need to ensure diversity, fairness and impartiality amongst magistrates, given that the English tradition of unpaid service is likely to continue for many years, if only because of its low cost. By the same token we need to know more about how the non-legal members of tribunals are selected.

Other Legal Workers

Finally, there are several groups of participants in the legal process who have received little attention from researchers or reformers. First, there are the staff of solicitors' offices and barristers' chambers. There is no Law Society or governmental requirement that solicitors must train their staff. Indeed the Royal Commission on Legal Services was opposed to a formal training rule claiming that matters would best be regulated by the market. If a solicitor provided a better service because staff were highly skilled, this would attract more business. This ignores the fact that many clients do not know what level of training an employee has nor would they be able to assess the significance of any particular qualification. There is an organisation which looks after the interests of solicitors' employees. It is called the Institute of Legal Executives and its main function is to provide part-time training for such persons. It has about 15,000 members and offers an integrated programme of study for school-leavers and other employees of solicitors. It has basic and more advanced examinations in both law and legal procedures which can be studied for at local colleges of further education on day release or in the evenings or by correspondence courses offered by the Institute itself. At times it shows the conflict between its role as a kind of trade union trying to get higher pay and, perhaps, some independent rights of legal practice for its members, and its need to support the general interests of solicitors who employ its members. It is not clear whether legal executives will attain a greater place within the legal system. One of the indications against this is the fact that the Institute is not arguing for a more significant role for its members as practitioners in their own right. Nevertheless it does not always see eye to eye with the Law Society.

Another group of lawyers comparatively neglected by writers on the legal profession are those employed in industry and by central and local government. We know their numbers (several thousand in the private sector and perhaps 4,000 in the public sector). What we do not know is their role in commercial and governmental decision-making. Are they asked for advice and is it followed? Or, when things go wrong, is it because they were not asked for advice in sufficient time or at all? This is particularly important in the public sector. When a Minister's or local authority's decision is overturned by the courts on judicial review we simply are never made aware of the importance departmental lawyers had in the process that led to the offending choice of options. We know about the routine work they carry out – drafting subordinate legislation, conducting litigation, preparing primary legislation (in conjunction with expert drafters known as Parliamentary Counsel) and undertaking conveyancing. They have consciously chosen to give up the usually high rewards of private practice for a secure but less well-paid life of serving one client only. We need to know more of the profiles of such lawyers.

Finally a very neglected group of legal workers are those many thousands employed within the courts. They have little or no legal training (except for the minor judges known as registrars or masters and clerks to magistrates who are legally qualified) yet it is on their shoulders that falls the responsibility for processing the large number of claims made. Automation and the use of computers have been very slow to be adopted as a means of speeding up the course of litigation. The review of civil procedure now under way will need to consider the function of court staff and see how their role might be adapted in an era of advanced technology.

Our forms of legal education and training have been changed slowly. What is needed is a radical review which will look at all aspects of the development of legal skills and abilities. Such a review is long overdue. The main factor pointing to delay in considering what should be done will be cost. Governments will not pay for improved training. The profession is also reluctant to pay more. As a result its entrants may be less able to deal with clients and their problems than they should be.

CHAPTER
4

THE NEED FOR LEGAL SERVICES AND THEIR COST

We have seen that the demand for legal services has increased greatly in recent years. The number of practising lawyers has expanded and the work available has risen for the economic and social reasons I have put forward. But all was not well with the comfortable world of conveyancers, commercial lawyers and company specialists. Briefly the complaints were that lawyers charged too much money, that they were pompous, remote from the problems of the majority of the population and neither willing nor able to deal with the range of rights supposedly assured by law to tenants, consumers and welfare recipients.

Such criticisms of the legal profession were first heard in the 1960s. They corresponded with other features of the social and political climate at that time. A number of politicians and academics (broadly associated with the Labour Party) had rediscovered poverty. They defined being poor not merely as having a low income in work or on welfare benefits but also being unable, through the deprivation of low material resources, to participate in society as a full member. Despite the fact that a system of legal aid had existed since 1949 lawyers were seen as unresponsive to the 'unmet legal needs' of the poor. It was pointed out that legal aid expenditure was, in practice, largely restricted to matrimonial work and crime. Lawyers and the legal system were not showing any signs of being concerned with the legal problems of poverty. The legal aid scheme was seen as inadequate to deal with such problems. There had to be change.

Legal Aid and Advice
It is impossible to understand the changes that have taken place within the legal profession without knowing how the legal aid and advice scheme developed, how it operates and what its short-

comings were. The scheme dates from 1949 and might be seen as one of the last developments to the post-war welfare state. Certain key decisions were taken then which have both produced the present system and are also a feature of some of its weaknesses and limitations.

The first principle adopted by the Legal Aid and Advice Act 1949 was that those who are unable to meet the costs of litigation should have free or subsidised (depending on their income and capital) access to the services of a lawyer and to the courts. In order to avoid legal aid work becoming a form of charity (as it largely was before 1949) these services should be provided by lawyers in private practice and the relationship between lawyer and client should be the same as for the privately paying client. The legal aid lawyer should be paid, as far as possible, at the same rate as if the client were solely responsible for the fees. Above all the delivery of legal services should be in the hands of the private profession. The Law Society was well placed to achieve these goals as it had been providing a limited form of free or subsidised legal services to those who had marital problems from the disruption caused by the last war. Indeed it was the Law Society's plan for legal aid that formed the basis for the 1949 Act. Although the scheme has been modified and improved quite substantially since then its basic components remain the same. It has been attached to the existing structure of the private profession and to the way in which costs are paid by parties to litigation.

Obtaining Legal Aid

To obtain legal aid to bring or defend court proceedings it is necessary to apply to a legal aid committee managed by the Law Society and composed of practising barristers and solicitors who have to apply a test of merits to the case. This involves asking two questions. First: 'has the applicant shown reasonable grounds for taking proceedings?' All that this means is whether or not, on the case as set out by the applicant, it seems that the claim to be brought or the defence put forward to someone else's claim stands some prospect of success. It is not necessary to show that the applicant will be bound to succeed or that the case involves large sums of money. However if the case is exceptionally complex (factually or legally) and the likely result will be the recovery of or payment of a small sum of money, legal aid might be refused on the second question to be answered, which is: 'is it reasonable to grant legal aid in this case?' While it is not common for legal aid to be refused on this ground it may tend to prevent an important 'test case' from being brought on legal aid where the claimant is trying to establish some general point of law but his or her financial interest in the outcome is small. Another example would be where the applicant's trade union can support the proceedings. In most instances where legal aid is available there is normally no problem meeting either test. For example, if a claim for compensation for personal injuries caused by another person's carelessness is made, it is usually enough to point to the way in which the accident occurred, the injuries suffered and an outline of the evidence available to prove the claim. In a more complex or uncertain case the committee might decide to limit the degree of assistance available to the obtaining of Counsel's opinion or the re-submission of the case to the committee after discovery of documents.

An inquiry into means is also necessary. This is carried out by the Department of Health and Social Security because of its ex-perience in assessing claims for social security benefits. The basic problem here is that for many years the financial limits were not increased in line with inflation so that it would be said that many people were too well-off to receive legal aid and yet not well-off enough to be able to afford the services of a private solicitor. There is no automatic rise in the financial eligibility limits in line with the cost of living index. However this problem has been taken more seriously in recent years and the government usually acts each year to increase the financial limits. At present what is called 'disposable income' must be below £5,500 a year. It is not gross income that matters but what is left after deductions are made. These cover tax and national insurance contributions, allowances for dependants, rates, interest on loans and so on. It is possible to have an income approaching £17,500 a year (well above average earnings) yet still be eligible for legal aid. Capital is also taken into account and, in general, must not currently exceed about £5,000. The value of a house is ignored but the income and capital of a spouse are taken as those of the applicant for legal aid. Legal aid may be granted at no cost or on payment of a contri-bution (which may be paid by instalments). Any contribution is fixed on a complex sliding scale.

Once a certificate has been granted it entitles the holder to the services of any solicitor or barrister willing to undertake legal aid work. Many large firms will not take on legal aid cases because they think that the rates of remuneration are too low and the process of claiming fees is too slow. This tends to limit the range of solicitors who will do such work to the smaller, sometimes less experienced or less well organised firms. Barristers of any seniority will usually take legal aid cases. If it is refused it is possible to appeal to the area legal aid committee but outright refusals on other than financial grounds are not common. It is usually necessary for solicitors to go back to the committee for authority to take unusual or potentially expensive steps such as employing the services of a Queen's Counsel.

Early in 1986 the government announced that an efficiency scrutiny of legal aid procedures would take place over a short period. Some practitioners saw this as a prelude to substantial cuts in expenditure even though, as we have seen, legal aid is underused by many who could benefit from legal advice. These fears were fuelled by a simultaneous cut in allowances against income for dependants given to those claiming legal aid. This seemed likely to increase the contribution required from many to whom legal aid might be granted. It would also distort the economics of solicitors who took on a lot of legal aid cases. No justification was offered for this cut other than the need to control expenditure.

A Legally Aided Case

When legal aid has been obtained the case is conducted normally. If the legally aided litigant is successful then the court will usually order the defendant to meet the bulk of the costs. If the claimant is not successful then he or she would not normally be ordered to pay the other party's costs but it is possible for a successful litigant against a legally aided party to have the costs met by the legal aid fund. However it must usually be shown that 'severe financial hardship' would be caused if the costs were not paid by the fund.

The Statutory Charge

In practice most legally aided litigants initiate claims and most succeed. But one special feature of the legal aid scheme will operate at the very moment of success. Any money or property recovered for the legally aided litigant is not immediately paid over. Instead it must be paid into the legal aid fund. If an order for costs is made these are assessed in the usual way (see below) and the money, if recoverable from the defendants, is also paid into the fund. The fund then pays the legal fees and expenses and recovers these from the money it has received. If, therefore, there is a shortfall, the fund will also take some, at least, of the costs paid out from the compensation paid to the legally aided litigant and from any contribution previously made.

At first sight it seems very unfair for compensation to be reduced in such a way. A person who cannot afford to finance the litigation seems to be penalised just for being of modest means. The reason is that the legally aided litigant should not be better off than the privately paying client. If a private payer succeeds in an action in the courts but cannot recover all the costs from the defendant, then he or she will have to pay the costs from the compensation awarded. The legally aided litigant is put in the same position. In effect legal aid is, at worst, an interest-free loan to cover the costs of the proceedings. At best it provides a guarantee against any risk for costs.

There is one case where the practice of the fund having a first claim on money or property recovered can work in an ususual way. Legal aid is available for matrimonial disputes, particularly as to property and financial claims and arguments about who shall have custody of the children. In such cases the income and capital of the spouse is ignored.

The value of any house owned by either husband or wife (or both) is also ignored. This means that very often both husband and wife can obtain legal aid, one to bring the claim and one to defend it. As the court has a wide discretion to do what it thinks best it will rarely regard one party as having 'won' and the other as having 'lost'. This leads to no orders for costs being made. If, for example, a wife receives a lump sum payment from her husband, the Law Society will impose a charge on the sum and use it to meet the costs. And if the husband is particularly perverse he may drag out the proceedings and run up costs which will admittedly have a cost for him but will also reduce the value of what his wife (and children) receive. If what is 'recovered' is a house or an interest in a house then the Law Society has a discretion to postpone the enforcement of its claim until the house is sold. Even then it may transfer the charge to any new home obtained especially where there are children. If money is 'recovered' there is no discretion to postpone enforcement and the Law Society takes its slice immediately to meet the costs. The only restriction on the operation of the charge in family cases is that the first £2,500 of any money (or equivalent value in a house or flat) is excluded. The reasons for this are obscure and the sum has not been raised for many years. It can be argued that it is illogical to ignore the value of a home when assessing a person's worth for legal purposes but to take account of it when the case has been successful. The important feature of the Law Society's charge is that clients should be aware of the potential impact of the charge and that, especially in family cases, it will reduce the sum recovered. It may operate as an incentive to settle at too low a figure because of the fear of costs biting into the amount eventually awarded by a court.

Costs

Let us look at costs more broadly before dealing with other aspects of legal aid. Fear of cost is one reason why the services of lawyers are not used as often as they might be. Cost involves not only the lawyer's fees but also the fees of a successful opponent. As a general rule the courts do not impose high charges for bringing a case. The average court fee in the High Court or County Court is about £50 to begin a case with a further fee sometimes being paid when the case is put in a list for hearing. A part of the cost of providing a court service comes from the fees but the remainder is met by the government from general taxation.

The real problem of costs is that the usual rule followed by the courts is to require the losing party to pay the winner's costs. Not all the costs can be recovered. It is only those that the court decides were reasonable and necessary. This has two results. First, a winning party cannot expect the loser to pay for extravagant conduct of a case. It is no good using a QC where a junior barrister could conduct the case perfectly well. But second, however frugal the winner has been in the conduct of the case there will always be some costs to be paid by him or her which cannot be recovered from the loser. In any event if the loser cannot or does not pay, there will be a problem about liability for the fees. If a client is not legally aided the solicitor will want money on account of fees not only at the beginning of the case but throughout. Towards the hearing date the solicitor will also want to be put in funds in order to pay the barrister's fees.

Criticising the Costs' Rule

The rule that the winner gets costs (at least some costs) from the loser has been both justified and criticised. In favour of the rule it is said that it discourages litigation and encourages the parties to settle. Costs are, in this sense, a deterrent to litigation but why do we wish to deter those with legitimate disputes from having them heard before the courts? If the answer is to prevent congestion of business then should we not spend more money on court buildings, staff and judges? If we believe, however, that litigation should be a very last resort why do we not take steps to provide simpler and cheaper methods of dispute resolution? A powerful criticism is that the rule is a very arbitrary device. A case may be won or lost on a technicality or on a very complicated point of law where the arguments would have gone either way. The courts normally only consider the result and not the history of the case in deciding who should pay the costs.

This problem of costs is particularly accentuated when cases go to appeal. The loser again pays the costs including the costs of the hearing in the lower court or courts. This is why very few privately paying litigants fight cases in the higher courts. Parties are either legally aided, are large companies or are part of central or local government. One device invented by the courts to reduce the burden of costs is 'payment into court'. This is a procedure allowing a defendant to pay into the court's accounts a sum of money to meet the claim. The claimant is told of the payment and has a short period within which to accept or reject the amount offered. If it is accepted the case comes to an end and the defendant must pay the costs up to the date of the payment-in. The claimant can reject the offer. But there is a great risk in doing so. If the case then goes to a full hearing and the claimant fails to obtain a judgment for more than the amount paid in, then he or she is regarded as having lost the case even though some money may be awarded. The awful result is that the claimant has to meet the costs from the date of payment-in which will be deducted from the money in court. This can mean that the claimant ends up with little or nothing by way of compensation. Even legally aided claimants are subject to this rule.

The system is most often used in personal injury litigation where the outcome of cases is so uncertain. The medical evidence may be unclear, fault by the defendant may not be easily proved and the judge will always have a discretion as to the precise amount of damages to be awarded. Almost all defendants in such cases are insured and the insurance companies have a shrewd idea as to how much to pay in to tempt a claimant to settle. This figure may be less than might be recovered by going on with the case but it may be more. The criticism made is that this turns the courts into a casino – a claimant has to gamble in a situation of great uncertainty. The justification for the practice is that it also enables a defendant who wants to settle to take something of a gamble and avoid the potential liability to meet a claimant's costs. The judge is not told about the payment-in and reaches his decision not knowing what amount, if any, is in court.

This practice is only well suited to claims for money. But it is creeping into other types of case. In matrimonial cases where a house may be at stake it is hardly possible to pay bricks and mortar into court! Instead it is possible to write a letter to the other party's solicitors stating a basis on which a settlement is acceptable. This can be referred to on the question of costs when the court has reached a decision on the dispute itself.

Although, as we have seen, tribunals hear many more cases than the courts, fees are rarely charged and costs are rarely awarded to either party. In some tribunals there is a power to award costs where one party has acted frivolously or unreasonably in bringing or defending a claim. This is sometimes used in Industrial Tribunals where a claim for unfair dismissal either has no basis or is so well founded that the employer should not have opposed it. It is arguable that a practice of not awarding costs or charging fees only transfers the expense from the parties to the case to the state. But this may be better than the whimsical system of payment-in and the possibility that a party to whom costs are no object can scare a moderately well-off but not legally aided opponent into settling for fear of costs.

Other Ways of Funding Litigation

It has been suggested that three methods of financing litigation should be considered which depart radically from the present pattern of legal aid or private payment. First, there is the contingency fee arrangement. This is a method of paying lawyers according to the result. If they fail they recover no costs or expenses from their client. If they are successful they are paid a percentage of the compensation awarded. This system is regarded with horror in this country. It is said that it gives the lawyers too personal an interest in the case and they lose their objectivity. But why is it that a lawyer may not be committed to the client's case in a personal way? It is also said that no such method of payment is open to defendants because there will be no sum of money recovered from which the fees can be paid. The answer to this is that it is claimants who are often disadvantaged by not being able to obtain legal aid for financial or other reasons yet not being rich enough to afford the costs of litigation. It is also said that lawyers tend to take a high percentage of an award in fees – at least, this criticism is made of lawyers in the United States where contingency fees are common. This might be controlled by limits on what could be charged. But at present no such method of payment is allowed here.

Another means of financing litigation is by legal insurance. This has been rather slow to develop in this country, given the existence of the legal aid scheme, and as with all insurance arrangements, there tend to be limitations and restrictions on the scope of the cover. Some attractions of insurance are the potential capacity for litigation it offers to those outside legal aid limits and, given that most defendants in personal injury and other accident claims will also be insured, the possibility of settlements being agreed faster by insurance companies between themselves.

A third method of limiting the cost of litigation has been suggested. There are cases where the argument turns almost entirely on a difficult point of law where the decision could go either way. Such instances are not very common but where they do occur the costs tend to be very high as the case may go all the way to the House of Lords. The rule that the winner receives costs from the loser seems particularly unfair where the result turns on a legal rather than a factual issue. Why should private parties have to meet the cost of resolving legal difficulties or ambiguities? Against this it is said that the litigants in such cases are either legally aided or are substantial corporations. In either case costs are not a problem. The proposal for a 'suitor's fund' which would finance such problematic litigation has not, therefore, found favour.

Curiously a minor variant on this idea has recently become a part of civil procedure. It has occasionally happened that during a very long case the judge has died. The case has had to be restarted and all the costs incurred by both parties on the first hearing have been wasted. One solution was for the litigants to insure the judge's life but this was difficult to arrange because there was little or no information about the judge's health. A way out now exists. The Lord Chancellor has recently been given powers under the Administration of Justice Act 1985 to meet wasted costs in such cases, although he only has a discretion to do so and not a binding duty. But the scheme is significant as being the first recognition of the need to meet some of the risks of litigation from public funds apart from legal aid.

Using Legal Services

The basic problem remains. Legal services in this country are under-utilised in those areas of law where rights have been given to the population, yet which need legal assistance in their enforcement. When it comes to property matters (conveyancing, wills, taxation and trusts) there is widespread use of lawyers. In those areas where subsidised or free legal aid is available, there is also high utilisation of lawyers. Divorce, criminal law and personal injuries are the most common examples. But in those areas of law where the rights of the poorest are in issue there is very little use made of legal services. Legal aid is not generally available for tribunal work so lawyers have little incentive to become experts in social security law, housing law or individual employment law. So the legal system appears unwilling or unable to deliver the rights that are given on paper. The commonest complaint made about lawyers is that their services are too costly and not accessible to many sections of the public.

In 1976 the then Labour government set up a Royal Commission on Legal Services to examine the nature of legal work in this country and to recommend changes that would be beneficial to the public. Its report in 1979 did not provide a blueprint for radical change. It preferred to rely on gradual measures which would have extended the scope of legal aid and the small but important public sector – law centres and the like. It is more recent events which have produced more rapid change which is by no means concluded in 1986.

In 1983 it became known that a solicitor, Mr Glanville Davies, had grossly overcharged a client. He submitted a bill for £197,000 which was reduced by the court on taxation (a procedure allowed to disenchanted clients) to some £68,000. Such an event could hardly have been a mistake. The Law Society has procedures for dealing with dishonest and fraudulent solicitors. It subjects them to disciplinary procedures and can take away their qualification or suspend them from practice. It has set up a compensation fund to ensure that no client loses money as a result of a solicitor's misuse of a client's funds. But in the Davies case it did little or nothing about the complaint. Mr Davies was at one time a member of the Society's governing body. Eventually the client had to find another solicitor and bring a case before the High Court to have Mr Davies struck off the rolls as a solicitor. A later inquiry by the Law Society into its own procedures showed an exceptional tale

of incompetence, mistakes and a total failure to come to grips
with the problem.

Another development was the move within the solicitors'
profession to do away with limitations on advertising. These had
long existed, partly to preserve the notion that solicitors were
altruistic, placing their clients' interests above profit. The breach
of the conveyancing monopoly was another blow to a practice
which has been particularly lucrative for solicitors.

Unmet Legal Need

Before looking to the future let us consider what the problems
were and are with the delivery of legal rights and how far these
have been overcome by changes up to 1986. The complaint most
commonly made was that lawyers were failing to meet legal need.
That is, rights apparently assured by law were going unenforced
and even unknown. Lawyers had failed to bring their services to
the attention of that part of the public which most needed them.

This argument was first heard in the late 1960s. It emphasised
that rights on paper were worse than useless and that ways had
to be found of making access to legal services cheaper and more
effective. Given that the legal process is best suited to dealing with
individual disputes rather than general problems of social deprivation, it was also seen as important to modify the form of legal
practice. One solution was to set up law centres or neighbourhood law firms which would serve the interests of cities where
traditional lawyers were not found, and which would be more
approachable and less exclusive than solicitors. They would be
funded by central government or local authorities and could
therefore undertake work free from the limitations of legal aid.
Their history and development has been very important and out
of all proportion to the number of lawyers working within them.

Problems of Legal Aid

Before we look at public sector legal services in more detail, we
need to consider how the private profession responded to criticisms of its inability to meet the needs of all those who had a claim
to legal services. The first line of attack made against it was to
point to the inadequacies of legal aid. It was not available for
tribunal work. Its income and capital limits were very modest and
had not been kept up to date with inflation. Moreover the exclusive and old-fashioned image of both solicitors and barristers was
not seen as suited to the modern age where the interests of the

consumer are seen as significant. Lawyers' monopoly of legal knowledge and the mystification which surrounds the law would be seen as dominating the client in whose interests the lawyer claimed to act.

The profession, particularly solicitors, answered these criticisms by seeking to increase the coverage and scope of its services. In 1972 it secured the passage of a new Legal Aid and Advice Act which was designed to fill an important gap left in the earlier legislation. In 1949 it had been intended to set up a scheme for legal advice which might prevent the need for litigation, or might, at any rate, enable those with problems in areas not traditionally associated with lawyers to obtain access to advice and possibly to have a solicitor deal with a problem in a way falling short of litigation. The plan was for salaried solicitors to give advice in centres all over the country run by the Law Society. In addition it was always the intention to extend the coverage of full legal aid to tribunals. Financial constraints and a wish by lawyers to get used to the innovative nature of the scheme in 1949 meant that these two proposals were never implemented. It is also a fact that during the 1950s lawyers in private practice were doing well enough providing traditional service and had little or no reason to look for new work. The Law Society no longer wanted to implement the 1949 scheme for salaried lawyers to give advice. It was only the rise in owner-occupation that led to an increased demand for property-based legal services. The expansion of higher education produced more solicitors and the profession came to see that it had a direct interest in expanding its areas of work. This led to some initial conflicts with law centres as will be seen, but the outcome was more opportunity for work within the private profession.

'Green Forms'

The 1972 Act enabled solicitors to provide an initially limited amount of advice and assistance following a simple means test for clients. Solicitors could administer this themselves and if they found that the limit on expenditure (currently £50, but more in matrimonial cases) had to be exceeded, they could apply to the local legal aid committee for an extension. This means of giving advice is usually known as the 'green form' scheme because of the colour of the simple form completed by the client. It can be used for any area of legal work although it does not permit representation before a tribunal or before a court. Experience has shown that most of the money available is taken up by family and criminal problems. In such cases it often leads to an application for full legal aid. Very little money has been spent on other types of legal problems such as housing, welfare rights or consumer complaints. A very limited variation in the green form scheme allows for representation in family cases heard by Magistrates' Courts, (which is becoming less common as divorce has become easier), representation of parents in care proceedings and applications by mental patients for release to Mental Health Review Tribunals. All governments have so far resisted pressure to extend this form of representation to other tribunals, entirely on the grounds of cost.

The Law Society took other steps to increase both the attraction of private practitioners to non-traditional work and the adoption by the public of such facilities. It did this by a campaign of collective advertising which stressed the nature of advice that lawyers could give. It also produced a series of referral lists giving the name and address of solicitors prepared to give advice on legal aid. It showed the subjects in which they professed a willingness to advise, but as no check was made on the solicitor's skill or competence in the area it was largely self-validating. However the lists were widely distributed and could be seen as an attempt both to obtain more work for lawyers and to encourage lawyers to venture into new areas. Initially advertising by individual solicitors was still not permitted but this rule was first relaxed in the early 1980s and by 1985 there were few restrictions on individual advertising.

The main concern of solicitors was to maintain and, if possible, increase the scope of legal aid work. This was to be done by treating the legally aided client in the same way as the private payer. That the problems of many poor people were and are different from those of the rich was not seen as important. Nevertheless the improvements to the legal aid scheme offered solicitors a new source of income and at least held out the possibility of advice being available to those who had not previosly been near a solicitor's office. The problem, however, is precisely that – people have first to identify their difficulty as having legal dimensions. If they do not, or if they do not know how to find a lawyer, then bigger and better legal aid schemes are of no help to them. All the evidence available shows that some fourteen years after the green form scheme began most clients of most solicitors are middle class individuals (or companies) with conventional legal needs which are met in a conventional way. This is not to say that a lawyer would be the panacea for many kinds of social and political problem. But if legal services were needed the feeling grew in the 1960s and 1970s that the private profession could not deliver the required provision.

Access to Legal Services

How then could the gap be filled? And did the poor need legal services anyway? The debate on these questions is by no means over. Historically the key pointer to the gap was the fact that so many rights were not being enforced or, worse still, even recognised by potential clients of legal services. Whether all problems having a legal dimension are capable of being solved by lawyers is more complicated. Take the case of a tenant (whether of a local authority or a private landlord) whose roof leaks. There is a vast amount of law on the topic. Without going into detail it is clear that in most cases the tenant will have an unanswerable claim to have the leak repaired at no cost. Indeed the law generally requires the landlord not to allow a leak to develop in the first place. But does the tenant necessarily have a legal problem? It may be that the landlord would like to carry out the work but has no money immediately available to do so. A local authority might have severe limitations on the cash it can spend. A private landlord might claim that the controlled rent paid is too low to enable major repairs to be done. The use of a lawyer might compel the landlord to carry out the work. But if it is not only one tenant but a group of tenants who have the same complaint, going to law on a case-by-case basis will be inefficient. The problem might even be described as a social or political one. Another view is that the use of legal services would even up the imbalance between the tenant or group of tenants and the landlord. A problem may have both legal and social or political elements.

There are other problems. Even if we say that the tenant with the leaky roof needs a legal service does it have to be provided by a lawyer? Could a Citizens' Advice Bureau, for example, not provide help and assistance and persuade the landlord to comply with the law? Alternatively as Phillip Lewis pointed out in a famous essay in 1973 (in *Social Needs and Legal Action*) the tenant might be better advised to obtain the services of a roofing contractor. Put more simply, 'the tenant might need a ladder and not a lawyer'. It all depends on the cost to the tenant (or to the legal aid fund) of legal services compared with the cost of hiring the roofing repairer. Of course, there is no simple mechanism for ensuring that public funds will pay for the cost of repairs rather than for the services of a lawyer and still less for recovering the cost from the landlord. But overall this might be a more efficient way of delivering legal rights.

The Royal Commission on Legal Services did some research and considered that there were two principal explanations for a low take-up of legal services in the area of welfare and consumer rights. First, there was the incomplete scope of legal aid, notably for tribunal work. Second, there was a lack of realisation by individuals that a legal solution might be appropriate or even available. This was often combined with a fear of high costs, a lack of understanding of where to obtain advice and an image of lawyers as not concerned with the problems of ordinary people.

Public Legal Services

These problems had been identified by others long before the Royal Commission began its work. The Law Society, as has been seen, at first promoted the idea of salaried lawyers giving advice in offices all over the country, but later abandoned this. It then favoured a variation on this idea. Liaison officers would be established in most cities and towns who would ensure that Citizens' Advice Bureaux and other advice agencies would serve as a link between solicitors in private practice and potential clients in need of legal advice. This would avoid the need for individual solicitors to promote their services by advertising and, at the same time, would produce more work for solicitors overall. In fact only one liaison officer was ever appointed and he worked from the Law Society's head office in central London. Events had overtaken the Society and a new idea was aired during the late 1960s. This was the publicly funded law centre.

The origin of the movement for a public sector in legal services was a curious conjunction of views by lawyers in both the Conservative and Labour parties in 1968. Each group of lawyers pointed to the inadequacies of existing legal services. The Labour lawyers wanted neighbourhood law firms to be set up broadly modelled on experiments in providing legal services in the United States outside private legal practice. The Conservative lawyers preferred to see more emphasis given to the private practitioner but thought there was some room for the creation of law centres on a limited basis, provided that they did not compete unfairly with the private practitioner.

Law Centres in Practice

The first law centre was opened in North Kensington in 1969. This was (and still is) a deprived area in London with many social problems. Since then about fifty such centres have been set up. They are funded in a variety of ways. Some get money from central government under urban aid programmes. Others are supported by local authorities with some money occasionally provided by major charities. The official response of the Law Society was not enthusiastic. Law centres were seen as taking away work from private practitioners, particularly from small or medium sized firms. This was a curious argument given that law centres did not want to do conventional legal work and posed no threat to conveyancing or other traditional legal services. The Law Society tended to make difficulties about requests by law centres to be allowed to advertise their services. It supported its attitude by insisting that the legal aid scheme, although not perfect, was a better basis for progress in legal services. It treated subsidised or non-paying clients in the same way as those paying privately. The Society saw law centres as offering a charitable and therefore divisive if not indifferent service.

As time went by the Law Society realised that law centres would do no harm to the private practitioner. On the contrary they tend to attract so much work that they cannot cope with it all and have to refer some to local firms. This is so, even though law centres generally concentrate on welfare rights and other areas of work such as juvenile crime or child care, not usually handled by solicitors in private practice.

Law centres differ greatly in their approach to the delivery of legal rights. Some concentrate on providing a service to individuals in the area of welfare rights, immigration and housing. Others prefer to deal with local community groups and see themselves as a legal resource in an essentially political struggle for improved social conditions. All are run by a management committee with strong representation by local interests. They are often open in the evenings and at weekends. Some employ social workers and other counsellors as well as qualified lawyers. Many pay their staff the same salary regardless of role or qualification.

Law centres are often concerned not only to use the law to its full effect but also to change the relationship between solicitor and client. Instead of the conventional pattern where the lawyer notionally 'takes instructions' from the client but in reality tends to dominate the relationship, the centre will look for greater equality between the two.

The Royal Commission was broadly in favour of the continuation and even the expansion of law centres. But it wanted them to limit the amount of group work they did in favour of offering a service to individuals. It thought that such work was too limited and might lead law centres into overtly political activities. In fact little or nothing has been done to implement these proposals and the future of some law centres looks rather uncertain as the government seems to have no firm policy for their continued funding or indeed for their future.

The government has also responded negatively to the Royal Commission's proposal for a 'Council on Legal Services' to be responsible for the management and supervision of both public and private legal services. All that has happened since 1979 is that the Citizens' Advice Bureaux seem to be handling more and more cases (especially in the field of welfare rights) and most bureaux now have excellent legal referral facilities. Some have trained their staff to undertake tribunal work, particularly in the case of employment law and social security claims.

It is unrealistic to think that the public sector will continue to expand or that legal aid will suddenly be extended to all tribunals or even to some. There are signs that the private profession is taking the provision of legal advice to the poor more seriously, even if this is prompted by intense competition in traditional areas like conveyancing. Organisations like the Legal Action Group with its concern to spread information about welfare law, its growing membership and its local branches encourage the more sophisticated use of legal aid in securing legal rights. Massive increases in state expenditure on legal aid are simply not on the political agenda. Better use of the funds that are available (which could include greater use of the green form advice and of salaried lawyers working in Citizens' Advice Bureux) seems to be the most likely outcome of current moves for improved legal services.

CHAPTER
5

THE CRIMINAL COURTS

Our society makes a distinction between conduct which is merely
a wrong under civil law and that which amounts to a crime. In
many cases both civil and criminal liability can be incurred. Take
the common instance of a road accident in which someone is
injured. There may be a crime – careless or reckless driving. It
all depends on who caused the accident and that person's degree
of fault in driving badly. There may be a civil wrong (a tort) if
negligence on the part of the driver can be proved. If criminal
proceedings are brought then the court that deals with the case
will not be concerned about compensation for the injured party.
Although in some other cases, as we will see, criminal courts can
award compensation here, the two procedures are quite different. This is generally explained on technical grounds. Civil and
criminal procedures differ. In criminal cases there is a higher
burden of proof on the prosecution than on the claimant in civil
cases. Criminal law is mainly concerned with the state's response
to prohibited conduct and not with compensating the victim.
Criminal courts have much greater involvement by non-lawyers
(magistrates and jurors) than do civil courts. (Tribunals are different as they often have non-legal members.)

The criminal law is usually thought of as dealing with major
offences against persons and property. This is true but very incomplete. Professor Glanville Williams says in the preface to his
massive and authoritative textbook on criminal law that a rough
summary of the cardinal principles would be: 'Refrain from violence and act honestly'. Of course, it is all more complicated than
that. When is violence permitted – in self-defence, in defence
of others, in defence of one's home or property, in assisting
the police? What is honest conduct and how is it to be judged?
The rules of the criminal law tell us much about these questions
although their application in any case will be for a jury or magis-

trates to decide. And whether a person is prosecuted at all will often depend on the exercise of discretion by the police. We will look at this in more detail later on.

The Content of the Law

Criminal law is a mixture of judge-made principles and Acts of Parliament. The older law shaped and created by the judges is often hard to state with precision although most cases do not turn on any point of law. The Law Commission has recently published a report setting out a draft code of the general principles of criminal law, but it is not yet known whether the government will implement it promptly or at all. Some specific areas of the law are also shrouded in uncertainty. In the last twenty years the House of Lords has considered the law of murder on several occasions. There is still doubt about precisely what mental element a person who has killed another must have to be guilty of murder rather than manslaughter. Previous proposals by the Criminal Law Revision Committee (another law reform body) for the codification of this branch of the law have not been passed into a statute. In one area of the law there has been a codifying statute. The Theft Acts 1968 and 1978 set out in a fairly comprehensive and comprehensible form the law relating to theft, burglary, blackmail, fraud and similar offences.

Over the years the courts have had to consider the meaning of the Act in a series of decisions, some of great complexity. The principles of the law are clear enough but their application in specific cases may give rise to problems. Take an example. Theft is defined as: 'dishonest appropriation of property belonging to another with the intention of permanently depriving the other of it'. Suppose that a dishonest person switches the labels on items in a supermarket intending to buy the dearer article for the cost of the cheaper one. Is this theft at all? If so, is it complete when the labels are switched or is it only complete when the items are taken to the cash desk? The courts puzzled about this for some time and eventually decided that the crime was complete at the earlier point. But there might not be an offence if the labels were switched as a joke or to cause confusion. Some would say that such marginal questions can safely be left to the higher courts.

Another view is that such issues should be clear from the legislation itself. Yet another opinion is that people whose overall behaviour is dishonest have taken a risk that they will be found to be criminals and no time need be wasted on discussing fine points of interpretation. The trouble with this view is that the law does not simply criminalise any dishonest conduct but only specifically defines forms of behaviour. A more basic difficulty is that the more complicated the law becomes, the more lawyers are needed to tell people what risks their conduct bears. Much the same is true of the civil law and it may be that simplification of the law is neither an easy nor an essential task. At any rate there is little sign that the criminal law is becoming simpler.

Criminal Procedures

The basic structure of the criminal courts is shown in the diagram on page 91. The vast majority of offences are tried in the Magistrates' Courts and the vast majority of defendants plead guilty. If this were not so the court system would almost collapse overnight. Likewise if every accused person said to the police: 'I'm not answering any questions and I'm not making a statement. If you think I'm guilty you prove it.', trials would be twice as long, the cost of legal aid would go up alarmingly and more barristers would be needed to represent defendants. In fact most defendants do not exercise their so-called 'right to silence'. This is the principle whereby the police have to prove their case beyond reasonable doubt and cannot force the defendant to help them. It is much hallowed as a civil liberty, but all the evidence is that it is rarely exercised in practice. Unless the accused person is a professional criminal (and therefore well used to police questioning), the pressures on a person isolated in a cell or interrogation room are all directed towards speaking volubly. The practical consequences of these pressures are partly recognised in the law. The Police and Criminal Evidence Act 1984 (which came into force on 1 January 1986) allows the police to detain persons after arrest and before charging them with an offence. There are various time limits laid down and in the case of serious alleged crimes the permission of a court is needed for prolonged detention. This is balanced by a general right of access to legal advice in the police station. Most lawyers would advise their clients on most occasions to say nothing. There is, however, a growing body of opinion which holds that there is an advantage in making a statement where the defendant denies the allegation and has a good defence. It can then be said at the trial that the defendant first raised the defence on the spot when questioned and not at the trial itself after many months to think it up. Whether this view prevails depends on the widespread use of tape-recorders in police stations. There have been

CRIMINAL COURTS

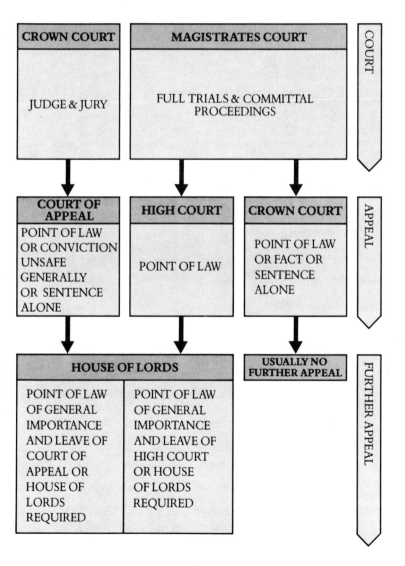

CROWN COURT	MAGISTRATES COURT		COURT
JUDGE & JURY	FULL TRIALS & COMMITTAL PROCEEDINGS		

COURT OF APPEAL	HIGH COURT	CROWN COURT	APPEAL
POINT OF LAW OR CONVICTION UNSAFE GENERALLY OR SENTENCE ALONE	POINT OF LAW	POINT OF LAW OR FACT OR SENTENCE ALONE	

HOUSE OF LORDS		USUALLY NO FURTHER APPEAL	FURTHER APPEAL
POINT OF LAW OF GENERAL IMPORTANCE AND LEAVE OF COURT OF APPEAL OR HOUSE OF LORDS REQUIRED	POINT OF LAW OF GENERAL IMPORTANCE AND LEAVE OF HIGH COURT OR HOUSE OF LORDS REQUIRED		

continual complaints that the police do not take down what
people say fully or at all. It is said that later two officers present
at an interview will produce a version of the questioning which
indicates guilt. Either answers would be invented, it was said,
or the interview record would omit answers favourable to the
defendant. Tape-recording would eliminate this but experiments
in the use of such machines have been slow to produce definitive
results. It seems that mandatory tape-recording will be introduced
later in 1986.

Another feature of police questioning and detention is the
problem of access to lawyers mentioned above. A duty solicitor
scheme has been established under the 1984 Act but a dispute
arose about the rates of pay. In early 1986 the scheme was not
fully operational, but, on paper at least, represented a substantial
increase in rights for suspects. It was the overall aim of the 1984
Act to strike a balance between the requirements of the police to
be able to interrogate and convict the guilty and the protection
of the innocent. It remains to be seen how this will work out in
practice.

The Decision to Prosecute

In most cases it is the police who decide whether or not to bring
charges. In some serious cases the papers must be passed to the
office of the Director of Public Prosecutions who decides whether
to bring charges. But it is not only serious cases where the
Director is involved, as under various statutes his consent is
needed before a prosecution can be brought. Since early 1986 the
conduct of all other prosecutions is to be in the new independent
prosecution service. But the 'Crown Prosecutors' will not decide
whether to charge a suspect in the first place. This will be left with
the police.

Many factors enter into such decisions. The individual police
officer who sees a minor motoring or other offence committed
may decide to caution the person involved but to take no formal
action. In other cases the decision requires a full consideration of
the evidence against the suspect and all the personal circumstances
of that person. These would include the health, age, previous
convictions (if any) and explanation offered by the suspect. The
views of the victim are sometimes taken into account, but there is
no method by which the victim can be formally involved in the
decision. Of all these factors the most important is whether the
evidence is sufficiently strong to give a reasonable prospect of

conviction. This is a question of judgment. Some people may be fortunate and escape prosecution. Others may be exposed to prosecution where the case is weak and should never have been brought.

Non-Police Prosecutions

It is still possible for private prosecutions to be brought but, apart from the case of quarrelsome neighbours, these are rare. What is more common is for a prosecution to be brought by a local authority health inspector or trading standards officer. The Health and Safety Executive also has powers to prosecute for a breach of safety regulations. Open any local newspaper and a report can usually be found of a prosecution of some hapless restaurant owner for having a dirty kitchen. There will usually be a long story behind the court hearing. The health inspector does not usually have to prove that the owner intended to commit the offence. It is usually referred to as a crime of 'strict liability'. But enforcement officials rarely use a prosecution as their first weapon. Rather they prefer to persuade and cajole the offender into improving standards leaving court action as a very last resort. Only where promises of compliance are made but not kept will a prosecution follow. The problem with this approach is that it leads to inconsistency between one area and another as to the point where a prosecution is begun.

Another device for limiting prosecutions is often used in fiscal offences such as tax evasion or smuggling of contraband (not drugs). Here the Customs and Excise or the Inland Revenue may extract financial penalties from offenders rather than prosecute. This saves court time and expense. But only those with money can avoid a prosecution. The person charged with fiddling while receiving social security will rarely be able to afford a penalty payment even if such an opportunity is offered. This seems to be discriminatory. But it is arguable that the offender who, in effect, buys off a prosecution will be under close surveillance from that time onwards and will have paid heavily for their offence. The public stigma of a prosecution is not present, however, and this may cause resentment by other (often lesser) offenders.

Defendants in the Criminal Process

Given that most offenders plead guilty in the Magistrates' Courts what can be said about the nature of the process they go through? Some can plead guilty by post – minor motoring offenders, those who have no television licence and those who have committed some other minor offence. Small wonder then there are often calls for such procedures to be formally extended to many other crimes. Fixed penalties could be imposed (as with parking 'tickets') and only if these were not paid would a prosecution follow. Such steps come close to de-criminalising conduct.

The whole problem with our criminal courts is that the same system is used for the trial of a murder charge (or other serious offences) and the trial of petty offenders. Take an example. A group of youngsters in a provincial town have too much to drink on a Saturday night. A fight breaks out. People are injured, property is damaged and a charge of affray is brought. This is a serious offence consisting of fighting in public so as to cause fear or apprehension by passers-by. The case can only be tried by a judge and jury. In such instances the magistrate only inquires briefly into the charges and makes sure that there is some sort of case. It goes on for months. The persons involved will usually have been reconciled. It may be that the public demands that something must be done. But is a prosecution before the Crown Court the answer? Should we not be thinking of other procedures – often called 'diversions from formality' – which would show society's disapproval but which would also deal with such offenders in a more suitable way?

There are signs that the cost of criminal justice may lead to such steps. Although there is no general right to legal aid in the Magistrates' Courts it can be made available where, in broad terms, the interests of justice demand it. There have been considerable variations in the way different courts approach the grant of legal aid. In some courts it is relatively easy to obtain whereas in others (often not far away) it is much more difficult on the same or similar facts. These discrepancies are partly reduced by the institution of 'duty solicitor'. This is a scheme whereby a local solicitor experienced in criminal cases attends court on a rota basis. Sufficient solicitors participate in the scheme for courts to be staffed on each day they sit. All defendants who have no legal representation can see the solicitor for advice. The case might be adjourned or it might be dealt with that day with the solicitor putting forward such mitigation as exists. Or the solicitor might apply for bail. For solicitors the scheme is a useful and legitimate way of obtaining legal aid work.

The Magistrates' Court in Practice

Many defendants do not seek legal advice and are (or seem to be) content to be passive spectators of events happening around them. They may be bewildered, confused, inarticulate albeit that they often guilty. The courts cannot stop for too long to see whether they really understand the procedures or whether they would be best served by legal representation. The routine process of getting through the cases means that the proceedings must carry on at a reasonable pace. In the Crown Court matters can be dealt with in a more leisurely manner with full representation for both the police and the defendant.

Legal aid is, in principle, available for hearings before magistrates. Preliminary advice can be obtained under the 'green form' scheme (see page 82), but this does not extend to representation in court. The defendant must pass a financial test and the court must be satisfied that 'it is in the interests of justice' that legal aid should be granted. The decision to grant legal aid can be granted by the clerk to the magistrates (a qualified lawyer), but only the magistrates themselves can refuse legal aid. A contribution may be required depending on the defendant's means.

Some defendants are entitled to legal aid as of right such as those facing a charge of murder or those held in custody after conviction pending sentence. For everyone else the rather uncertain test of 'the interests of justice' may lead to some inconsistency in granting or refusing legal aid as between one court and another. In an attempt to clarify the generalities of the scope of the test some criteria have been laid down to guide the courts. They include:

the gravity of the charge

whether any difficult question of law arises

where the defendant will have difficulty in following the proceedings, e.g. because of mental illness

where there are witnesses to trace and interview or where police witnesses will have to be cross-examined by an expert

the desirability of representation in the interests of someone other than the defendant, e.g. where there is a charge of a sexual offence against a young person who should not be cross-examined by the accused in person.

A limited right of appeal exists against refusal of legal aid. This only applies where the case could be heard in the Crown Court but in fact is to be heard before magistrates. (The defendant can often choose to have cases such as theft or lesser charges of violence heard in the lower Magistrates' Court.) The local legal aid committee can grant legal aid if it chooses. Little is known about this procedure as it has only been in operation for about two years, but there is some evidence to show that the success rate on such appeals is quite high. The duty solicitor scheme is another means of ensuring that defendants get some representation.

Both legal aid and the duty solicitor's scheme provide a means for representing the accused before magistrates. Governments have always resisted a right to representation in all cases for reasons of cost. As with tribunals this places a heavy responsibility on the courts to ensure that an unrepresented defendant is treated fairly and justly.

The Jury System

We know very little about how jurors operate and how they reach decisions. Great faith is placed in the jury and lawyers usually advise those clients who have the choice of trial before a judge and jury to choose it. Magistrates are often thought to be too prosecution-minded. Juries are thought to be less ready to accept police evidence.

Most of this has no factual basis. It is not lawful to investigate jury decision-making by sitting in on their deliberations or asking jurors questions after the trial is over. There is little evidence to show that juries acquit too many guilty offenders or convict too many innocent persons. And how many would be too many given that some mistakes will occur in any system? Many acquittals arise because the judge so directs. In such instances the prosecution turns out to be weak or to suffer from some fatal evidential flaw. Juries are allowed to disregard what the judge tells them about the law and to acquit even in the face of the evidence if they do not like the fact that a prosecution was brought. This is a valuable safeguard against oppressive prosecutions as the recent case of Mr Clive Ponting might be taken to show. But it is rather capricious in nature. Some of our institutions with time-honoured origins do not stand up to very close examination, even if that were possible in the case of juries. It does not follow that all alternatives are illiberal or worse than the unknown quantity represented by juries.

A recent proposal for some major and very complex fraud cases to be tried by a judge with a panel of experts rather than a jury has been generally greeted with derision. Again it must be said that such an option is at least worth exploring if there is no other way of dealing with complicated allegations about criss-crossing accounts and elaborate fraudulent devices.

Ways of Looking at Criminal Courts

Writers and researchers on criminal law and procedure have tried to develop ways and means of making sense of complex processes. The two most common models or images of the system are those described by Herbert Packer, an American criminologist, as the '*due process model*' and the '*crime-control model*'. The first stresses the need for the rights of defendants to be paramount and for the right of silence to be maintained. The prosecution must prove their case strictly. Evidence of previous convictions of the offender will generally be disallowed as too prejudicial. Some guilty persons may, as a result, be acquitted but the innocent should always go free.

The other model places more emphasis on the need to control crime and to restrict technical defences. The defendant must (expressly or implicitly) displace a presumption of guilt. The police should be given the means to combat crime. Given that most offenders both confess and plead guilty there is little need for elaborate procedural rights. And if the police do not always respect the rights of suspects this shows that such rights are often not in the interests of law enforcement.

English law and procedure tends towards the first model in theory but to the second in practice. It may be that the prosecution must always prove guilt, but it usually happens that a defendant on trial needs to offer some explanation of what happened to stand a chance of being acquitted. And if 'plea bargaining' (pleading guilty to the offence charged or, often, to a lesser charge in return for an implied understanding of a lighter sentence) reduces the courts' workload, has anyone suffered?

The main point is that the due process model rarely explains what happens in practice. It is clear that the system could not cope if all suspects had a full-length trial. We do not know whether we need to change the system itself to cope with such matters or whether the idealised version of a lengthy adversarial contest is best preserved as a formal basis of justice in the relatively few cases where it is actually used. In the next few years it is likely to be pressures of cost which lead to less formality and more diversion from formal procedures, but no greater number of full trials.

CHAPTER
6

DEVELOPING THE LAW

We have seen that the law develops partly as a result of decisions by the courts (the 'common law') and partly by successive governments passing legislation. Sometimes this legislation is part of a clear political programme. The present Conservative administration has made many changes in the laws concerning trade unions and the rights of employees. It promised to do so in its election manifesto. Previous Labour governments have made changes in the same area of law and so it is not likely that this legislation will have a long life.

The two methods of changing the law are interrelated. It is for the courts to interpret a piece of legislation and say what its words mean. For example, an Act was passed in 1975 to control the practice of allowing guard dogs to roam freely about warehouses and other similar premises. There had been cases of people being attacked by such dogs when calling for a legitimate reason. The Act made it an offence to have a guard dog on premises unless:

'. . . a handler who is capable of controlling the dog is present on the premises and the dog is under the control of the handler at all times . . . except while it is secured so that it is not at liberty to go freely about the premises.'

This provision is ambiguous. It may mean that a dog can only be used to guard premises when a handler is present who has control of the animal. If the handler has to leave the dog it must be tied up but the handler must stay on the premises. Alternatively it may mean that the dog may be left on the premises without a handler provided it is tied up. The ambiguity arises because the exception comes at the end of a long sentence and it is not clear whether it applies to the entire provision or just to that part dealing with a guard dog which is tied up while the handler is somewhere else on the premises.

Such an ambiguity cannot be resolved merely by reading and re-reading the words of the provision. The courts do not allow reference to be made to *Hansard* (the report of debates in Parliament) because they have long thought that the words of the Act are paramount rather than the intention politicians hoped to give to them. (But the judges can 'cheat' by looking up *Hansard* for themselves.) Because this provision imposed a criminal penalty, when its meaning came before the courts they said that the ambiguity had to be resolved in favour of the citizen. Therefore it was held to be lawful to leave a dog on premises tied up but with no handler present. How closely it had to be secured was a question of degree in each case, depending on the size of the premises and the length of rope or chain. After the case that decided this point, the law was not changed by the government so we may assume that the interpretation the court placed on the provision was correct. To avoid this sort of problem the Law Commission recommended in 1969 that all statutes should have an explanatory memorandum with them to explain their purpose which could be used as a guide to interpretation. This proposal has still not been acted upon.

It is open to any government to change the law either by directly moving to alter the result of a particular case or to codify an existing area of common law. Neither step is usual today. The result is that to know what the law is on any topic it is necessary to look at case law, at any relevant Acts of Parliament and at the interpretation placed on these by the courts. One of the functions of the Law Commission is to keep the whole of the law under review and to bring forward proposals for the reform of those areas of law that have not kept pace with changes in society. A recent example is the detailed draft of a criminal code which would replace much confusing and complex case law by clear statements of principle, which, it is hoped, will not become encrusted with subsequent decisions interpreting these statements. It remains to be seen whether this proposal will be passed into law.

The Common Law in Action

There are two principal areas of law where the main sources of the legal rules are found mostly in cases rather than in Acts of Parliament. These are the law of tort (from the identical French word meaning 'civil wrong') and the law of contract. The most important tort is that of negligence, which in broad terms provides compensation for those who suffer losses or injury as a result of the careless action of somebody else. Put in this simple way the basic rule is stated clearly enough. But it has to be further refined to be of much use either as a standard for deciding future cases or as a predictor to lawyers as to how their clients may fare if they bring or defend a legal claim.

Most claims are brought by individuals who suffer damage whereas most defendants are, in practice, insurance companies standing behind the person who committed the wrong. In some cases both parties are, in reality, insurers. What tends to happen is that the insurer of the property will pay out where, for example, a factory has been damaged by the careless act of a builder on the adjoining land. The insurer then looks around to see who is responsible and brings an action using the name of the insured to recover the money paid out.

To see how the law of negligence has developed (and to see how adequate it is today) we need to look at some history. The modern law is only just over fifty years old. In 1932 a very important case came before the courts. It was a case taken to the House of Lords on appeal from Scotland. The claimant wanted compensation because of what had happened one hot day in a café in Paisley. Mrs Donoghue wanted a drink. With a friend she went into a café owned by Mr Minchella. Her friend bought her a bottle of ginger beer. The bottle was made of dark opaque glass. She drank some of the contents thinking it was pure ginger beer. When she poured herself a refill she alleged that the decomposed remains of a snail floated out. She claimed that she suffered shock on seeing this disgusting object and that she suffered from gastro-enteritis as a result of consuming the first portion of the drink. As she had not bought the drink herself she had not made any kind of contact with Mr Minchella and had no claim against him. She therefore brought an action against the manufacturer of the drink, a Mr Stevenson, who had also bottled it. She claimed that he was careless in his manufacturing process and that he should have used a system of work which prevented harm occurring to consumers from impurities in the contents of the bottle.

Such a claim may not seem very startling today when we often hear of claims for huge sums of money as a result of some careless act by a doctor or even a lawyer. But in 1932 it was significant because, before then, no general principle of liability in negligence existed where no contract could be established. It was clear by then that someone injured as a result of a road traffic accident could bring an action. Indeed the courts had been used to dealing with 'running down' cases involving horses, stagecoaches and hansom cabs for many years. But nobody had previously tried to sue a manufacturer for harm caused by a defective product not dangerous in itself. The case proceeded on the questions of law and no finding on the facts was ever made.

The case established two principles. First, a careless manufacturer of a dangerously defective product is liable to a consumer who suffers personal injury. Secondly, and more important for the future, a wider doctrine emerged. This was the idea of 'a duty of care' owed by all those whose products or activities might reasonably be foreseen as likely to cause harm to others. This broad principle could only be given a more precise meaning and application in later cases. The case itself was settled out of court for £100 so we do not know whether there was a snail in the bottle or not! What is particularly significant is that successive governments have not intervened in the development of the law except, as we shall see, in specific areas for very particular reasons. One result of this decision to leave the shaping of the law to the courts has been to require individual or corporate claimants to bring new actions before the courts to test the limits of the law. The cost of such actions might be paid by the legal aid fund, or more probably, by insurers who have met the cost of commercial claims and wish to recover what they have paid out. Each of the later milestone cases have been very fully argued and have generally reached the House of Lords. This is a very good illustration of the importance to the legal system of the advice given by senior barristers as to what points can fairly be argued at any particular time (see pages 33–34 for a discussion of this point).

The Development of the Law

A number of questions were left open within the broad principle of *Donoghue* v. *Stevenson*. Was the type of harm for which compensation could be given restricted to physical injury (as happened in the case itself), or might it include economic or financial harm? Even if this went too far would it include shock and distress rather than some clearly measurable physical injury? And what about harm caused by those who fail to act and cause loss or damage? In the case itself Stevenson could positively be said to have caused the harm alleged. In later cases claims were brought against those who merely stood by and failed to prevent harm occurring.

It is now clear that in some cases claims for pure financial loss

are recoverable. In 1963 an advertising agency was able, in principle, to obtain compensation for a careless reference given by a
bank as to the financial standing of one of the bank's customers.
The agency proposed to give it credit. It lost the case on the facts
because the terms of the reference excluded liability for errors by
the bank. The House of Lords stressed that they were not necessarily allowing claims to be brought for all types of economic
harm. The bank had a special relationship with the agency and the
harm had been caused by words alone rather than by an act. In a
later case in 1973 the Court of Appeal declined to give full compensation to the owners of a factory which suffered losses when
builders carelessly cut through an electricity cable and interrupted
the supply to the factory. The factory made steel and alloys and
the management had to damage the contents of a furnace in order
to prevent more damage to the furnace itself. In addition it was
unable to process four sets of alloys which caused a loss of profit.
The court readily awarded compensation for the damage to the
furnace but would not allow the claim for loss of profits. The
court thought that physical damage consequent on the careless act
was recoverable but the loss of profits represented a hazard which
the factory owners had to face themselves. It pointed out that
there would be no end to such claims, some of which would be
inflated or even bogus. Insurance could easily or cheaply be taken
out and it should not be possible to pass on such losses to contractors or even to the electricity board itself.

Some doubt was thrown on this case by an important case in
the House of Lords in 1983. Here a warehouse owner employed a
firm of builders to carry out major works. The flooring work was
subcontracted to specialist floor-layers who did the job badly.
Nobody was injured but the whole floor had to be taken up. While
this was being done the warehouse could not operate and a large
claim for loss of profit was made as well as for the cost of relaying
the floor. The warehouse owners could have made a claim for
breach of contract against the main builders. But they chose to sue
the subcontractors in negligence. To the surprise of many commentators the claim succeeded. It was within the broad principle
of *Donoghue* v. *Stevenson*. True, it was mainly a claim for loss of
profits, but the relationship between the warehouse owners and
their subcontractors was particularly close. It is not yet clear how
far this decision goes because in some later cases the courts have
backtracked to some degree and have hesitated to recognise a very
broad concept of liability for economic loss.

Some other cases decided a few years ago remain good law. In 1970 the Home Office was held liable for failing to prevent some Borstal inmates from escaping and causing damage to yachts in a nearby harbour. There was a powerful argument based on policy grounds that there should not be any liability. This contended that Home Office officials would be less willing to experiment with minimum security methods of dealing with inmates if mistakes would cost their employers large sums for compensation to those whose property was damaged. The courts brushed these aside by saying that modern penal methods were compatible with a duty to take care to prevent inmates from escaping.

The Role of Government

There are Acts of Parliament dealing with aspects of negligence. But they only concern peripheral areas where the common law had posed particular problems which the case law had not solved. For example, in 1957 an Act was passed rationalising the liability of occupiers of land towards lawful visitors. Another Act was passed in 1984 dealing with liability by such occupiers to trespassers. In 1976 an Act was passed allowing a child born disabled to bring an action for a careless act which caused injury yet which was committed before the child was born. In common law no such claim had ever been admitted. The advantage of legislation here was that it could deal with all the problems involved in imposing such liability. A case or series of cases cannot achieve this because such decisions of the courts spring from the particular facts. For example, the 1976 legislation (the Congenital Disabilities (Civil Liability) Act 1976) deals with the difficult question of whether a parent's action which contributed to the disability suffered by the child should lead to a reduction in the damages. The Act says that it does. A case would be unlikely to deal with such a point of detail.

None of these Acts deal with the greatest criticism mounted against the tort of negligence which is that it is often hard to prove that another person was at fault (see page 36). This raises more overtly political questions than much of the law of negligence. Would it accord with commonly accepted notions of morality to allow full recovery where the claimant was partly at fault? Should a defendant, even if insured, be held liable without fault? It is not only lawyers who can or should answer such questions.

A good example of governmental intervention in the common law lies in the area of consumer protection. For many years the 'small print' in contracts between business and consumers had posed problems of fairness. Consumers might find that they had signed away all their rights. The courts were initially not sympathetic, tending to adopt uncritically the old idea of 'freedom of contract'. This held that that however unequal the position of consumer and seller might be in practice, in theory the contract was freely entered into and ought to be enforced. Gradually the courts recognised the inadequacy of this approach. By various means they tried to limit the scope and effect of 'small print' clauses excluding liability. First, they often found that the clause was not part of the contract. For example, in one case a hotel tried to rely on an exclusion clause contained in a notice found in the guest's bedroom. The guest's property was stolen due to the hotel's lack of care which was a breach of contract. The court had no difficulty in holding that the contract was concluded at the reception desk so any later introduced clause was of no effect.

Secondly, the courts interpreted the clauses very strictly. Unless the clause was clearly wide enough to exclude all liability the courts would say that the clause was not effective to limit or exclude liability for breach of contract. For example, in one case a car was destroyed by fire while in a garage for repair. There was a wide exclusion clause, but, as the fire was caused by the carelessness of the garage, the court decided that it was not wide enough to cover what had occurred.

These methods of protecting consumers were limited because, sooner or later, the users of 'small print' clauses ensured that they were included as part of the contract and that they did cover the breach in question. The response of the courts was to develop a much broader doctrine which said that some breaches of contract were so serious that no exclusion clause could cover what had occurred. This doctrine proved quite useful in protecting consumers but it collapsed in the 1960s when the House of Lords reasserted older ideas of freedom of contract. Finally the government intervened. In 1973 it became impossible to exclude liability for most breaches of contract between sellers of goods and consumers under the Supply of Goods (Implied Terms) Act. Goods had to be of a reasonable quality and fit for their purpose.

In 1977 this idea was taken further with the Unfair Contract Terms Act. Some other unacceptable exclusion clauses were made invalid. In particular those excluding liability for death or personal injury were struck down. These were very common in the case of car parks or other places containing some element of danger.

Most other exclusion clauses are made subject to a test of 'reasonableness'. This is a vague doctrine and has produced little case law so many lawyers advise their clients to settle such cases and not to litigate over matters of great uncertainty. But it was a doctrine the courts had failed to formulate for themselves. They now have sufficient flexibility to distinguish fairly negotiated exclusion clauses from those that are oppressive and harsh. This interplay between government and the judiciary and the transfer to the courts of complex issues of judgment is an interesting example of a pragmatic solution to a difficult problem.

A Summary: The Courts and Parliament

Much of our law remains in the hands of the courts. In some areas, such as taxation, social security and much of our commercial law, the basic rules are found in legislation but the courts have to interpret these laws. Law reform is essentially a political as well as a legal task and the Law Commission has not, in general, consulted very widely about its proposals for change in any given area of law. Equally the courts are not well equipped to make major policy changes in the law based on argument springing from one case. But it is important to notice that the process of changing and developing the law is a complex and dynamic one with different roles played by Parliament, the courts and the Law Commission. The latter is a permanent body (with a judge as Chairman) charged with keeping the whole of the law under review. Some of its work is in very technical areas of law but most of it deals with those complex areas of land law, family law and property law generally where there is a great need for clarity and redrawing of the law in modern terms. It prepares working papers (on which it invites comment), then issues a final report.

Most of the Law Commission's recommendations have been enacted into law but that law is not thereby made more accessible to the population at large. Moreover it has generally been kept away from politically controversial areas of law such as labour and trade union law, constitutional law and administrative law. In one area of interest it recently tried to consult very widely. This concerned the reform of the law relating to the contracts of young people under eighteen. (In general such contracts are not enforceable.) It sent working documents to many schools although it did not conduct any kind of hearing. It may be that, in future, it will adopt a more open style of reforming the law. Certainly, law reform is too important to be left to lawyers alone.

CHAPTER
7

THE USES OF LAW

It is clear that in recent years the public has made more demands of law and lawyers. Law is often seen as a solution to all kinds of social problems, and opponents in political debates all place great value on legal mechanisms. Take the difficult question of urban deprivation, riots and social unrest. Those who see the issue as one of law and order wish the police to be given more powers. Some extension of police authority would be achieved by administrative measures but changes in the law of search and seizure or entry to private property would also be advocated. Those who see the issue as one of social problems caused by high unemployment and racial tension might argue for reducing police powers, increasing police accountability at a local level and more powers to local authorities to combat poor housing. All of these would require legislation to set up the necessary structures. And once established, constant reference would have to be made to the law to check that powers given were being properly exercised.

Many more examples of the use and expectations of law could be given. In the consumer area there is a growing awareness of existing rights and moves to give the public greater rights against sellers of shoddy goods or those who provide poor quality services. There are often calls for the creation of new criminal offences. When a disturbed man gained access to the Queen's bedroom at Buckingham Palace there were immediate moves to make trespass a criminal offence which, in general, it is not. A similar development occurred in 1977 when an elaborate law was passed to criminalise some forms of squatting. The legislation has hardly been used and is a supreme example of an assumption that passing a law is a simple solution to a difficult problem. We might say that the demands for more law are not always met by the practical operation of that law once it has been passed.

Some Examples

In some areas the use of the law (and therefore of legal services) has been quite marked in recent years. One example is the area of medical negligence. Twenty years ago law suits against doctors or hospitals were almost unknown. The difficulties of proving that someone was at fault and the cost of the proceedings for those not on legal aid were both important reasons for not pursuing claims. Also there may have been a tendency to accept that harm caused within hospitals was a pure accident. A doctor could say to a family, one of whose members had died after a routine operation: 'There's always a risk. Anyway these things happen. It's all very complicated – you wouldn't understand.' Clearly not all doctors would say this. But some might. Professionals are held in less awe today than they were and such words might not readily be accepted. We have seen a rise in the number of claims against hospitals and doctors and their insurance premiums have risen as a result. Yet other research into personal injury litigation has shown that many valid claims for compensation in road traffic and employment cases are not pursued. This is mainly because of the problems of getting access to legal advice discussed in Chapter Four. It is also a result of the procedural difficulties in bringing claims before the courts.

A disinclination to use the law and legal procedures is not limited to individuals. There is evidence that businessmen (who have very ready access to legal services) often do not pursue their full legal rights. Contracts are either drawn up in an informal manner or, where formal documentation is used, strict legal rights are not insisted upon. Orders might be cancelled without the seller asking for compensation for lost profits. Such a claim can usually be made in law. Equally buyers did not often insist on compensation for late delivery or even for defective goods. Where a long-term relationship existed between the buyer and seller it would be seen by both as futile to resort to law. Any problems could be sorted out by adjustments to later and continuing arrangements. Moreover legal procedures took up too much time and were costly. The priority is to retain working relationships and to avoid the formal and antagonistic steps involved in court proceedings. Legal action will be taken over bad debts but here there is unlikely to be any continuing or long term relationship. Also the legal proceedings are straightforward and not very expensive.

Plea Bargaining

Another example of the avoidance of formal procedures is in the prosecution of criminal offences. Not only do most offenders plead guilty but a process of negotiation often takes place between prosecution and defence for a plea of guilty to be accepted to a lesser charge than was brought. At one time the judge hearing the case would indicate that a reduction in sentence might be offered in return for a guilty plea. In particular the judge might become a party to the bargain by pledging that a custodial sentence would not be imposed if a guilty plea were tendered but that it might be if the defendant pleaded not guilty and were eventually convicted. This practice has been strongly condemned by the higher courts and appears no longer to be followed. There is an obvious risk of undue pressure being placed on a defendant to plead guilty where there is a good (or at least arguable) defence. There is a large literature on the topic which shows what these dangers are and how they might be avoided. The main point is that lawyers will normally be involved where the purpose of their taking part in the negotiations will be to limit the use made of formal legal procedures.

Another example in the criminal field is the use of discretion by the police not to prosecute. We are all familiar with the police officer who allows the speeding motorist to continue after a warning. The use of discretion is an inevitable and even desirable part of law enforcement. Even if there has been (or appears to be) a breach of the law it may not be appropriate to bring a prosecution because of the circumstances of the case. But the motorist may have learned as much of a lesson (if deterrence works at all) as if there had been a prosecution. In this and in the instances of the diversion from civil law we see, in part, a desire to save money and also a recognition that there are other methods of regulating behaviour of a less formal, yet often effective nature. Attempts to regularise such practices are rarely worthwhile and ignore the fact that law (and lawyers) may be too crude a way of affecting human conduct.

Is there any general lesson to be learned here? The limits of the law as a means of regulating society is a topic much considered by sociologists. In modern societies law is frequently used as a way of expressing and enforcing certain basic values. This approach often leads to a polarised dispute between two individuals who may yet prefer to settle their dispute outside the legal arena. Where the state is one party to the dispute it prefers to have tribunals resolve the matter rather than the ordinary courts. And where a particular collective problem is tackled by legal means we do not always find a very successful outcome. Some examples may be given. Prohibition in America is usually seen as a failure because it did not work. Too many people were prepared to break the law both in consuming alcohol and in providing it for others. A modern example is the debate over Sunday trading laws. Restrictions were to have been swept away partly because the present law is widely disregarded and has little popular support. However, the measure did not get sufficient support in Parliament. It will be interesting to see whether more prosecutions follow.

But are laws which are not adhered to worthless for that reason alone? Many laws are broken yet we do not suggest that they should therefore be repealed. Most people support the criminal law yet frequently break it, albeit in minor ways. We have, as motorists, all parked on yellow lines. As office workers we have all used our employers' paper clips or photocopier for our own purposes although tacit approval may have been given in some cases. Prohibition may have failed because the opposition to it was organised and the prospect of abolition was always a live option. But to enforce the law fully would have required massive interference with personal liberty. This would have troubled even the supporters of prohibition. What has never been fully explained is how the law ever got passed at all.

Discrimination and the Law

Another use of law that may eventually be more successful is the recent use of legal machinery to limit and ultimately remove all forms of racial and sexual discrimination. Here the law is primarily designed to affect behaviour. It does not necessarily seek to change attitudes but rather to prevent their expression from constituting discriminatory practices. This may, in the long term, reduce prejudice. It is also interesting to see that enforcement of the law is partly in the hands of aggrieved individuals who have all the familiar problems of access to law and legal advice. But it is also partly under the control of powerful bodies (the Commissions for Racial Equality and Equal Opportunities) which have the power to investigate allegations of discriminatory behaviour by organisations. This can achieve far more than one or even a series of individual cases fought through tribunals and courts. Of course, discrimination in the important areas of jobs and housing has not disappeared. Some writers argue that this is because of the nature of the basic structure of our society. Not only is there economic inequality but racial and sexual disadvantage are also an expression of social division and attitudes. It is no good preventing discrimination in employment if there are no jobs. The law cannot affect fundamental divisions in society, it is said. Perhaps not, but it can produce changes in behaviour among those who have to make vital decisions in employment, most of whom are rational beings and would not wish to discriminate.

There is then, a strong future for law and not only as a regulator of disputes in traditional areas of private relationships. The law of contract and commercial law generally (as one example) will continue to develop to meet the needs of modern society. But there will also be room for the use of law on a collective basis. For example, to control discrimination or to seek a balance between police powers and individual freedoms.

The Legal Profession Reformed?

If this trend continues then the legal profession will come under increasing scrutiny. Is its structure and organisation suitable for a modern society? The Law Society clearly thinks that it is not. In early 1986 it released details of a far-reaching proposal to change the form of legal practice. No doubt partly motivated by the breach of the conveyancing monopoly, it wants to blur the distinction between barristers and solicitors. This would produce more work for those who are now qualified as solicitors. The plan is for all lawyers to have common training at both the academic and practical stages. Only after some years as a general practitioner would a person choose to become a specialist advocate and take further examinations. This would preserve the Bar but in a modified form. It would be smaller than it is now and there would be no restrictions on rights of audience in any court. If a client wanted to be represented only by a general practitioner then this would be possible. In heavy cases a specialist advocate would almost always be required but in most cases the degree of expertise needed would be possessed by the general practitioner.

It seems that the Bar was not formally consulted about these proposals. But it is sensible to assume that there have been informal conversations not only between the Law Society and the Bar, but also with members of the government. Even if the plans are not implemented immediately or in full they have an attraction for a government opposed to restrictive practices. It has also the long-term advantage that if it is no longer necessary to employ both a barrister and a solicitor in every case there may be long-term savings in legal aid. The Law Society did not put any such proposal to the Royal Commission on Legal Services, but then it did not expect to see the conveyancing monopoly broken – the Royal Commission was against this.

There are some crucial questions to be answered before these proposals can be fully assessed. The most important is that of cost. Who will pay for the new system of common training and what form will courses take? Will support for trainees be available by mandatory local authority awards or will the profession have to put up the money by means of a training levy? Will the government meet any capital costs if training courses are to be provided by and within hard-pressed educational institutions? It is too early to predict the outcome of the consultation process in which the Law Society is now engaged. But it is clear that change far more radical than anything seen for generations is firmly on the political agenda.

The attitude of the Bar is unclear. Many senior members will be opposed to change. But their position is unlikely to be greatly affected. They will continue handling large cases. Junior members, on the other hand, will find much to their liking. Instead of having to wait for their fees which are now paid on a case-by-case basis they could become well paid salaried or profit-sharing lawyers. The present system of payment is grafted on to the existing professional structure and is often absurd in its operation. A barrister specialising in criminal work is likely to receive the greatest part of his or her fees from public funds whether defending on legal aid or prosecuting for the police. How inefficient it is for fees to be assessed for each case, instead of a retainer being paid. It is often said that the present system reinforces the independence of the barrister but, as we have already seen, nobody suggests that judges are not independent because they are paid a salary by the state.

Some small firms of solicitors will worry that the reduction in size of the Bar could have serious consequences. The argument is often put that every firm, small or large, now has access to the specialist advice and advocacy offered by the Bar. How far would this continue to be available? It is hard to answer this question. Small firms would probably have to merge and become more specialised or, at least, able to offer some more specialist services than they currently do. There would also be some transfer or referral of clients from one firm to another. And the present system is hardly the most desirable if by specialisation we refer to advocacy. It is no secret that the Bar's very short training in advocacy has to be supplemented by learning 'on the job', and this mostly takes the form of handling small cases in the County and Magistrates' Courts. (Whether the client always sees the case as 'small' is often not asked – the answer is only too obvious.) At any rate there is no reason to think that access to specialist advice would be less available than under the present system.

Just as this book was going to press the Bar and the Law Society announced that a joint committee had been established to look at all possible ideas for reforming the professions. The committee has an independent chairman and will contain non-legal members. It is to report within two years. The chairman strenuously denied that the creation of the committee was simply a way of shelving problems and postponing solutions. It remains to be seen whether such a committee, with many opposing views represented, will reach conclusions which are not merely very general compromises. What is interesting is that both the Law Society and the Bar recognised that something had to be done to allay public criticisms and to meet the demands for better and more accessible legal services.

Reforming the Legal System

For the present, the legal system continues in the way described in this book. In particular we have seen that the ideals of adequate representation, full participation in the legal process for litigants and the right of all to a full hearing are not always met. Legal assistance and advice is not always available. Most litigants do not play a full part in the handling of their cases. And most cases do not go to a full hearing but are disposed of in a summary way. Either no defence is entered (and we cannot assume that there will always be no defence) or the case is settled – not always on the best possible terms. This may undermine the ideal of due process of law. Discussing this point, Robin White, in his recent book, *The Administration of Justice* (Blackwell, 1985), says:

> '. . . the application of due process must be extended to include not just the final adjudication of a dispute but also every preliminary stage leading up to adjudication. This requires a broadening of the ideals of due process. The key must be the requirement at every stage that those involved in the process make choices freely and on an informed basis.'

In order to make such choices it is essential that a person without the knowledge, without the awareness of information to make such a choice has access to an independent adviser. Yet there will always be a danger that advisers, if they are professional lawyers, will come to dominate their clients' decision-making. At present it is unlikely that the legal aid fund would meet the cost of lengthy meetings or correspondence with a client in order to make freedom of choice into a reality.

Robin White goes on to propose two methods of making access to justice a meaningful exercise of civic rights. First, he argues that there is room for introducing more lay participation at all levels of adjudication. He takes the tribunal as a model with its legally qualified chairman and two lay members. He would like to see this form of dispute resolution extended to all lower criminal and civil courts. The lay members would ensure that the proceedings do not become so formal that the litigant cannot understand what is happening. The lawyer would ensure that the correct legal principles are applied. To avoid the lay members becoming too 'professional' their period of office could be limited both in time (to, say, five years) and in quantity (say, one adjudicatory body at a time).

This is a fascinating and stimulating idea. The government is currently reviewing the whole of civil procedure with the object of reducing costs, delay and complexity. It is not clear whether radical ideas such as these discussed here will be on the agenda. A more likely outcome will be the merger of the High Court and County Court with all cases starting in the County Court, no matter how large the amount involved. Only the most complex cases would be transferred to the High Court. This would achieve some administrative simplification and savings of costs, but would be unlikely to increase participation in the litigious process. Another possibility is the introduction of 'class actions' which would enable all those affected by a wrong (e.g. defective drugs) to bring a collective action to obtain compensation. Another problem to be faced is the inadequate level of representation and advice for litigants. An immediate extension of legal aid to tribunals seems unlikely, but there does seem to be room for other solutions. Robin White proposes three immediate steps. First, the number of law centres needs to be increased and their financial future secured. Second, there is an argument for a publicly funded service of lawyers who would be salaried and would conduct litigation in both civil and criminal proceedings. Third, paralegals (Citizens' Advice Bureaux workers, legal executives, and other consumer advisers) would assist with small claims and tribunals.

These far-reaching ideas need to be considered carefully. It is quite unrealistic to think that the law can be so simplified as to do away with the need for legal services. There needs to be more awareness of legal rights. An interesting project is now under way in selected schools for teaching law as part of the curriculum. This is sponsored by the Law Society. The cynic would see this as the equivalent of a bank offering a clipboard and pen to students in order to attract their custom for life. Perhaps the search for new work is the motivation of official representatives of solicitors. But it would have the advantage of increasing knowledge about the law in a serious way.

Other changes in approach by solicitors are welcome. The Law Society now has wider powers to control poor quality work by solicitors and to order the return of fees. The Lay Observer is an independent watchdog over the Society's handling of complaints against solicitors. It seems increasingly likely that the investigative and disciplinary functions of the Society will be transferred to a new body which will operate outside the Law Society. This would avoid any conflict between its role as 'trade union' and drummer-up of business for solicitors and the supervision and control of errant practitioners.

Human Rights and the Law

One recent move for increased use of law and lawyers is the Bill introduced by Lord Scarman for the enactment in English law of the European Convention on Human Rights. This would enable aggrieved citizens to challenge any law or administrative practice before our own courts as offending against the Convention. Instead of having to go right through the English courts and then wait years for a decision from Strasbourg, a litigant would raise the issue here. The Convention would be overridden by express language but, short of this, all laws could be scrutinised.

There is no doubt that this would greatly increase the volume of litigation. Professor Griffith does not believe that our judges are able or qualified to deal with broad issues of social policy encompassed in the Convention. In particular he thinks that the judges could not improve the quality of life for individuals if they had to interpret the broad provisos to the rights mentioned which, as some examples, allow restrictions on rights which are:

'. . . necessary in a democratic society in the interests of national security . . . for the prevention of disorder or crime . . . or for the protection of the rights and freedoms of others.'

He believes that judges are too closely linked to established authority to protect the public as a whole. His colleague at London University, Professor Zander, does not agree. He thinks that the overall result of enacting the Convention into English law would be to improve human rights. Even if the judges are basically conservative (with a small 'c') they would, in the long run, become used to dealing with broad concepts and principles. They would educate themselves as well as the rest of society, as time went on.

Yet other commentators wish to see an improvement to the delay and cost of taking cases to Strasbourg but would stop short of involving English judges in the breadth and depth of the Convention. The government is opposed to Lord Scarman's measure and it will probably not make much progress – at least for the moment. But Scarman and his supporters will not give up and a change of government might lead to a more sympathetic response.

Conclusion

This debate about more legal rights is only one part of the rapidly changing development of legal processes. Solicitors are under pressure. So is the Bar. Lawyers generally are looking for more work. Citizens are more aware of their rights and are making more demands of both lawyers and the law. There will be more changes to the legal system within the next five years than there have been for the last fifty. These matters are too important to be left to lawyers alone. If this small book has contributed in some way to a greater awareness of legal issues, it will have achieved its purpose.

APPENDIX

a

Ward v Tesco Stores Ltd

COURT OF APPEAL, CIVIL DIVISION
MEGAW, LAWTON AND ORMROD LJJ
13th NOVEMBER 1975

b *Negligence – Duty to take care – Breach of duty – Burden of proof – Evidential burden –
Accident not one that would ordinarily have occurred if defendants had complied with duty –
Absence of explanation by defendants showing that they had complied with duty – Defendants
owners and managers of supermarket – Duty to keep floors clean and clear of spillage –
Customer slipping on yoghourt spilt on floor – No evidence how long yoghourt had been on
floor or whether defendants had had reasonable opportunity to clear it up – Whether judge*
c *entitled to infer that defendants in breach of duty in absence of explanation by them.*

The defendants owned and managed a supermarket store. While shopping in the
store, the plaintiff slipped on some yoghourt which had been spilt on the floor and
was injured. She brought an action against the defendants claiming damages for
personal injuries allegedly caused by the defendants' negligence in the maintenance
d of the floor. It was not suggested that the plaintiff had in any way been negligent
in failing to notice the spillage on the floor as she walked along doing her shopping.
At the trial the defendants gave evidence that spillages occurred about ten times a
week and that staff had been instructed that if they saw any spillages on the floor
they were to stay where the spill had taken place and call somebody to clear it up.
Apart from general cleaning, the floor of the supermarket was brushed five or six
e times every day on which it was open. There was, however, no evidence before the
court as to when the floor had last been brushed before the plaintiff's accident.
The plaintiff gave evidence that three weeks after the accident, when shopping in
the same store, she had noticed that some orange squash had been spilt on the floor;
she kept her eye on the spillage for about a quarter of an hour and during that time
nobody had come to clear it up. The trial judge held that the plaintiff had proved a
f prima facie case and that the defendants were liable for the accident. The defendants
appealed, contending that the onus was on the plaintiff to show that the spillage
had been on the floor an unduly long time and that there had been opportunities
for the management to clear it up which had not been taken, and that unless there
was some evidence when the yoghourt had been spilt on to the floor no prima facie
case could be made against the defendants.

g

Held (Ormrod LJ dissenting) – It was the duty of the defendants and their servants
to see that the floors were kept clean and free from spillages so that accidents did
not occur. Since the plaintiff's accident was not one which, in the ordinary course
of things, would have happened if the floor had been kept clean and spillages dealt
with as soon as they occurred, it was for the defendants to give some explanation to
h show that the accident had not arisen from any want of care on their part. Since the
probabilites were that, by the time of the accident, the spillage had been on the
floor long enough for it to have been cleared up by a member of the defendant's
staff, the judge was, in the absence of any explanation by the defendants, entitled to
conclude that the accident had occurred because the defendants had failed to take
reasonable care. Accordingly the appeal would be dismissed (see p 222 *b* to *j*, p 223 *g*
j and p 224 *a* to *e*, post).
  Dictum of Erle CJ in *Scott v The London and St Katherine Docks Co* (1865) 3 H & C
at 601 applied.
  Turner v Arding & Hobbs Ltd [1949] 2 All ER 911 approved.
  Dictum of Devlin J in *Richards v W F White & Co* [1957] 1 Lloyd's Rep at 369, 370
explained.

Notes
For the burden of proof in actions for negligence, see 28 Halsbury's Laws (3rd Edn)   *a*
73-75, paras 75, 76, and for cases on the subject, see 36 Digest (Repl) 140, 141, *735-746*.

Cases referred to in judgments
Richards v W F White & Co [1957] 1 Lloyd's Rep 367.
Scott v The London and St Katherine Docks Co (1865) 3 H & C 596, 5 New Rep 420, 34
    LJEx 220, 13 LT 148, 11 Jur NS 204, 159 ER 665, Ex Ch, 36 Digest (Repl) 145, *772*.   *b*
Turner v Arding & Hobbs Ltd [1949] 2 All ER 911, 36 Digest (Repl) 57, *310*.

Cases also cited
Byrne v Boadle (1863) 2 H & C 722.
Dollman v A & S Hillman Ltd [1941] 1 All ER 355, CA.
Stowell v Railway Executive [1949] 2 All ER 193, [1949] 2 KB 519.   *c*

Appeal
This was an appeal by the defendants, Tesco Stores Ltd, against the judgment of his
Honour Judge Nance given in the Liverpool County Court on 21st February 1975
whereby he ordered that the plaintiff, May Ward, should recover damages of the defendants damages of £178·50 for personal injuries received when she slipped and fell   *d*
while shopping in the defendants' supermarket at Smithdown Road, Liverpool, on
29th June 1974. By consent the sum awarded was reduced to £137·10. The facts
are set out in the judgment of Lawton LJ.

David Owen for the defendants.
N Dugdale for the plaintiff.   *e*

LAWTON LJ delivered the first judgment at the invitation of Megaw LJ.   This
is an appeal by the defendants from a judgment of his Honour Judge Nance given
in the Liverpool County Court on 21st February 1975, whereby he adjudged that the
plaintiff should recover against the defendants £178·50 damages and her costs on
scale 2, for personal injuries said to have been caused by the negligence of the defen-   *f*
dants in the maintenance of the floor in their supermarket at Smithdown Road,
Liverpool. By consent the sum awarded has been reduced to £137·10. The higher
figure was due to an arithmetical error.
    On 29th June 1974, at about midday, the plaintiff went to the defendants' super-
market. It is a large one and is carried on in premises which used to be a cinema.
Inside, the premises were laid out in the way which is usual nowadays in supermarkets.   *g*
On duty there was a total of about 30 to 35 staff; but in the middle of the day that
number was reduced because staff had to be relieved in order to enable them to
get their midday meals.
    The plaintiff went round the store, carrying a wire basket, as shoppers are expected
to do in supermarkets. She was doing her shopping at the back of the store when
she felt herself slipping. She appreciated that she was slipping on something which   *h*
was sticky. She fell to the ground, and sustained minor injuries. She had not seen
what had caused her to slip. It was not suggested, either at the trial or in this court,
that she had in any way been negligent in failing to notice what was on the floor as
she walked along doing her shopping. When she was picking herself up she appreciated that she had slipped on some pink substance which looked to her like yoghurt.
It was yoghurt. Later, somebody on the defendants' staff found a carton of yog-   *j*
hourt in the vicinity which was two-thirds empty.
    A member of the staff helped to pick the plaintiff up. The manager was called.
The plaintiff was taken to his office. She was dealt with there in a kindly and con-
siderate way. The defendants offered to, and did, arrange for such of her clothes as
had been soiled by the fall to be cleaned.

a That is all the plaintiff was able to prove, save for one additional fact. About three weeks later when she was shopping in the same store she noticed that some orange squash had been spilt on the floor. She kept an eye on the spillage for about a quarter of an hour. During that time nobody came to clear it up.

The trial judge was of the opinion that the facts which I have related constituted a prima facie case against the defendants. I infer that this case, which involves only a small amount of damages, has been brought to this court because the defendants are
b disturbed that any judge should find that a prima facie case is established merely by a shopper proving that she slipped on a supermarket floor.

At the trial the defendants called some evidence. Their manager spoke about the store and how many staff were employed. He went on to say that the staff had the following instruction about spillages: 'Stay where the spill has taken place and call someone else.' He said that usually in a store of this kind and size there was to be
c found some member of the staff near where the spillage had occurred. He went on to say that the store had a system for keeping the floor clean. Contractors came in every night to give it a general clean-up. Twice a week those contractors carried out 'buffing', which in the south of England would be called 'polishing'. The manager said that every day whilst the store was open the floor was brushed five or six times. The defendants did not call any evidence as to when the store floor had last been
d brushed before the plaintiff's accident. It follows that there was no evidence before the court as to whether the floor had been brushed a few moments before the accident, or an hour, or possibly an hour and a half. The court was left without any information on what may have been an important matter.

The manager in cross-examination said that spillages did occur from time to time; he thought there were about ten breakages a week, but most of them came from
e the breaking of squash bottles

It follows that those in charge of the store knew that during the course of a working week there was a likelihood of spillages occurring from time to time. It was accepted at the trial that shoppers, intent on looking to see what is on offer, cannot be expected to look where they are putting their feet. The management should have appreciated that if there are patches of slippery substances on the floor people are liable to step
f into them and that, if they do, they may slip. It follows too that if those are the conditions to be expected in the store there must be some reasonably effective system for getting rid of the dangers which may from time to time exist. The only precautions which were taken were, first, the system of having the floor brushed five or six times during the working day and, secondly, giving instructions to the staff that if they saw any spillage on the floor they were to stay where the spill had taken place
g and call somebody to clean it up.

The main complaint of the defendants in this case has been that the trial judge should never have taken the view that the plaintiff had proved a prima facie case. It was submitted before this court that it was for the plaintiff to show that the spillage had been on the floor an unduly long time and that there had been opportunities for the management to clean it up which they had not taken. In support of that
h proposition, counsel for the defendants invited our attention to *Richards v W F White & Co*[1]. It is necessary to say something about the facts of that case because, as in all cases of negligence, the facts are important. A dock labourer who was working on a ship in dock which was being unloaded slipped on a patch of oil and injured himself. At the material time between 300 and 400 men in various trades were working on the ship. In the course of his judgment Devlin J said[2]:
j
'If there had been evidence which showed that there was some danger, not perhaps of oil but some other danger, which was being left on the ship for two or three days, or anything of that sort, which the shipowners were doing nothing

about, a *prima facie* case of negligence would be made out; but to make out a *prima facie* case of negligence in a case of this sort, there must, I think, be some *a* evidence to show how long the oil had been there, some evidence from which it can be inferred that a prudent shipowner, who had a reasonable system of inspection for the purpose of seeing that dangers of this sort were not created, ought to have noticed it.'

That case was decided on its own facts. I doubt whether Devlin J intended to make any general statement of principle. If he did, I would not agree with what he *b* said. This case, too, has to be decided on its own facts, to which established principles must be applied. The relevant principles were enunciated in the classical judgment of Erle CJ in *Scott v The London and St Katherine Docks Co*[1]:

'But where the thing is shewn to be under the management of the defendant or his servants, and the accident is such as in the ordinary course of things does *c* not happen if those who have the management use proper care, it affords reasonable evidence, in the absence of explanation by the defendants that the accident arose from want of care.'

In this case the floor of this supermarket was under the management of the defendants and their servants. The accident was such as in the ordinary course of things does not happen if floors are kept clean and spillages are dealt with as soon *d* as they occur. If an accident does happen because the floors are covered with spillage, then in my judgment some explanation should be forthcoming from the defendants to show that the accident did not arise from any want of care on their part; and in the absence of any explanation the judge may give judgment for the plaintiff. Such burden of proof as there is on defendants in such circumstances is evidential, not probative. The trial judge thought that prima facie this accident would not have *e* happened had the defendants taken reasonable care. In my judgment he was justified in taking that view because the probabilities were that the spillage had been on the floor long enough for it to have been cleaned up by a member of the staff.

The next question is whether the defendants by their evidence gave any explanation to show that they had taken all reasonable care. The only explanation which they gave was that to which I have already referred. The judge weighed the evidence *f* and decided as a matter of fact from which in this case there can be no appeal that the precautions taken were not enough, and that the plaintiff in consequence had proved her case. In coming to that conclusion he followed the judgment of Lord Goddard CJ in *Turner v Arding & Hobbs Ltd*[2]:

'The duty of the shopkeeper in this class of case is well established. It may be *g* said to be a duty to use reasonable care to see that the shop floor, on which people are invited, is kept reasonably safe, and if an unusual danger is present of which the injured person is unaware, and the danger is one which would not be expected and ought not to be present, the onus of proof is on the defendants to explain how it was that the accident happened.'

It is clear from a later passage in his judgment that Lord Goddard CJ, in referring *h* to the burden of proof, was not saying that the defendant had to disprove negligence. What he had intended to say is apparent from what he said later[2]:

'Here, however, I think that there is a burden thrown on the defendants either of explaining how this thing got on the floor or giving me far more evidence than they have as to the state of the floor and the watch that was kept on it *j* immediately before the accident.'

The learned judge had that passage in mind when he decided as he did. In my judgment he was right; and accordingly I would dismiss this appeal.

1   (1865) 3 H & C 596 at 601
2   [1949] 2 All ER 911 at 912

ORMROD LJ. I have the misfortune to disagree with the judgment of Lawton LJ.
a Starting from the beginning, I do not think that it was established that this accident
was caused by any want of care on the part of the defendants. The accident described
by the plaintiff—and she did no more than describe the accident, namely that she
slipped in some yoghourt which was on the floor of the supermarket—could clearly
have happened no matter what degree of care these defendants had taken. The
crucial question is how long before the accident the yoghourt had been on the floor.
b Had some customer knocked it off the shelf a few moments before, then no reasonable system which the defendants could be expected to operate would have prevented
this accident. So I think that the plaintiff fails at the outset.

So far as the proposition which Lawton LJ has cited from Erle CJ[1] is concerned, all
I would say is that, since this accident could quite easily have happened without any
want of care on the part of the defendants, I do not think that that broad proposition
c is applicable.

I for my part am unable to distinguish this case in any material respect from the
judgment of Devlin J in *Richards v W F White & Co*[2], to which Lawton LJ referred.
The learned judge put the matter in the clearest possible terms[3] in the passage
which Lawton LJ has read. I cannot improve on that statement of the law, and
would not attempt to. It seems to me quite clear that unless there is some evidence
d as to when the yoghourt got on to this floor no prima facie case can be made against
these defendants. I would only add that to hold otherwise would seem to me to
put on the defendants a wholly unreasonable burden, not only of care, but also of
proof. I ask myself what evidence could they have called? It would have been
fortunate, perhaps, if they had been able to show that their sweeper had passed over
this bit of the floor five minutes before the accident. But it would not have shown
e that their system was either better or worse than if the sweeper had gone by that
bit of the floor an hour earlier. And I cannot think that the case would have been
carried any further by calling evidence from such employees as may or may not
have been about. This is a supermarket, not a place with counters and assistants
behind the counters. I cannot imagine what evidence they could give except to say
that they had not noticed the spill; and the matter would have been taken no
f further.

For those reasons, in my judgment counsel for the defendants' submission is right,
and I would allow the appeal.

MEGAW LJ. I agree with the conclusion expressed by Lawton LJ, and with the
g reasons given by him for that conclusion. But as unfortunately the court is not
unanimous I feel that it is desirable that I should add a few words of my own, not,
I believe, in any way departing from the reasons given by Lawton LJ.

It seems to me that the essence of the argument put forward on behalf of the
defendants in this appeal is this. Never mind whether the defendants had any system
of any sort to protect their customers against the risk of slipping on the floor of the
h supermarket as a result of breakages or spillages, which on their own evidence
happened about ten times a week. Even if they had no system of any sort to guard
against such a risk to their customers, nevertheless, when an accident happens such
as the accident in this case, a lady customer who undoubtedly slips, through no fault
of her own, on such a spillage on the floor, she cannot recover against the defendants.
And why can she not recover? Because she is unable to prove that the spillage did
j not take place within a matter of a few seconds before she slipped and fell on it:
so that, however perfect a system the defendants had had, it would not have enabled
them to prevent this particular accident.

1 *Scott v The London and St Katherine Docks Co* (1865) 3 H & C 596 at 601
2 [1957] 1 Lloyd's Rep 367
3 [1957] 1 Lloyd's Rep at 369, 370

With great respect to those who support that proposition, it appears to me to be contrary to the law as I understand it to be. It is for the plaintiff to show that there *a* has occurred an event which is unusual and which, in the absence of explanation, is more consistent with fault on the part of the defendants than the absence of fault; and to my mind the learned judge was wholly right in taking that view of the presence of this slippery liquid on the floor of the supermarket in the circumstances of this case: that is that the defendants knew or should have known that it was a not uncommon occurrence; and that if it should happen, and should not be promptly *b* attended to, it created a serious risk that customers would fall and injure themselves. When the plaintiff has established that, the defendants can still escape from liability. They could escape from liability if they could show that the accident must have happened, or even on balance of probability would have been likely to have happened, irrespective of the existence of a proper and adequate system, in relation to the circumstances, to provide for the safety of customers. But, if the defendants *c* wish to put forward such a case, it is for them to show that, on balance of probability, either by evidence or by inference from the evidence that is given or is not given, this accident would have been at least equally likely to have happened despite a proper system designed to give reasonable protection to customers. That, in this case, they wholly failed to do. Really the essence of counsel for the defendants' argument—and he did not shrink from it—was: 'Never mind whether we had no *d* system at all: still, as the plaintiff has failed to show that the yoghourt was not spilt within a few seconds before the accident, she must fail.' As I have said, in the circumstances of this case, I do not think that the plaintiff, to succeed, had to prove how long it was since the defendants' floor had become slippery.

I take the view that the decision of the learned judge in this case is fully in line with the decision of Lord Goddard CJ in *Turner v Arding & Hobbs Ltd*[1], which has *e* been cited by Lawton LJ. Indeed, I am unable to see how, consistently with that decision, on the facts and the evidence here the learned judge could have reached any other conclusion.

As regards the decision of Devlin J in *Richards v W F White & Co*[2], to which Lawton LJ and Ormrod LJ have referred, I agree with Lawton LJ that that case has to be looked at in relation to its very special facts. When the learned judge said: *f* 'but to make out a *prima facie* case of negligence in a case of this sort, there must, I think, be some evidence to show how long the oil had been there', I am confident that he did not intend to lay down any general principle. It is, to my mind, not a part of the law, as I have said, that in this case the plaintiff must fail merely because she is unable to disprove that the yoghourt fell on the floor within a few seconds of the time that she trod on it. *g*

I agree that the appeal should be dismissed.

Appeal dismissed.

Solicitors: *A W Mawer & Co*, Liverpool (for the defendants); *Sharpe Pritchard & Co*, agents for *E Rex Makin & Co*, Liverpool (for the plaintiff). *h*

Mary Rose Plummer   Barrister.

---

1 [1949] 2 All ER 911 at 912
2 [1957] 1 Lloyd's Rep 367

BOOKLIST

ABEL, R. (Ed.) *The politics of informal justice* (2 vols) Academic Press, 1982.

ATIYAH, P. *Law and modern society* OUP, 1983

BERLINS, M. and DYER, C. *The law machine* Penguin, 1982.

BIRKINSHAW, P. *Grievances, remedies and the State* Sweet and Maxwell, 1985.

BROPHY, J. and SMART, C. (Eds) *Women in law* Routledge and Kegan Paul, 1985.

GRIFFITH, J. *The politics of the judiciary* Fontana, 1985 (2nd edn).

JOSEPH, M. *Lawyers can seriously damage your health* Published by the author, 1985.

KING, M. and MAY, C. *Black magistrates* Cobden Trust, 1985.

LEWIS, P. MORRIS, P. and WHITE, R. *Social needs and legal action* Martin Robertson, 1973.

MOLYNEUX, M. (Ed.) *Your guide to the law* Secker and Warburg, 1986 (3rd edn).

PRITCHARD, J. *The Penguin guide to the law* Penguin, 1986 (2nd edn).

ROZENBERG, J. and WATKINS, N. *Your rights and the law* J. M. Dent, 1986.

THOMAS, P. (Ed.) *Law in the balance: legal services in the 1980s* Martin Robertson, 1982.

WHITE, R. *The administration of justice* Basil Blackwell, 1985.

WILLIAMS, G. *A textbook of criminal law* Stevens, 1983 (2nd edn).

ZANDER, M. *Case and materials on the English legal system* Weidenfeld and Nicolson, 1985 (4th edn).

ZANDER, M. *The law-making process* Weidenfeld and Nicolson, 1986 (2nd edn).

Acknowledgement is due to the following

THE CONTROLLER, HER MAJESTY'S STATIONERY OFFICE for extract from *Supplementary benefit*: Claims and payment regulations: Statutory instrument 1981 No. 1525 published by the D.H.S.S. BUTTERWORTH & CO. LTD for the case of *Ward* v. *Tesco Stores* from the *All England Law Reports* (Volume I).

INDEX